GRACEFULLY BROKEN
Tragedy To Triumph

Steve Denton

Copyright © *Steve Denton*, 2025

All Rights Reserved

This book is subject to the condition that no part of this book is to be reproduced, transmitted in any form or means; electronic or mechanical, stored in a retrieval system, photocopied, recorded, scanned, or otherwise. Any of these actions require the proper written permission of the author.

TABLE OF CONTENTS

DEDICATION 1

INTRODUCTION 2

THE EARLY YEARS 3

ANARCHY IN THE UK 8

SCHOOL'S OUT 15

GROWING UP! 21

MUSIC MAKES THE WORLD GO AROUND 28

DAWNING OF A NEW ERA 33

FROM THE RISING OF THE SUN 40

...TO THE GOING DOWN OF THE SAME 44

FEMALE FRIENDS 49

YOU NEVER KNOW WHAT'S AROUND THE CORNER 53

HALF A CENTURY ON PLANET EARTH 57

IT MUST BE LOVE 62

AMAZING GRACE 67

WHAT'S SO FUNNY ABOUT PEACE, LOVE AND UNDERSTANDING 73

CONCLUDING THOUGHTS 74

DEDICATION

I have heard it said that losing a loved one can leave us without meaning to our life or having our sense of purpose but in my case that is not necessarily true. Some sixteen years ago I met a woman who went on to be first my friend, then my lover and eventually my wife. She died two weeks before the first anniversary of our marriage and, as heartbreaking as that is, I hope to share the joy and inspiration she left me with. This is dedicated to her, Angie, my hun.

INTRODUCTION

We often say "I'll never forget you" or "I'll never forget this" and whilst that is largely the case I wonder what it is that makes us remember certain people or moments in our lives. The following is an account of mine. I have intermingled memories of friends who appear in my story, memories of theirs that they have been kind enough to send me. I consider myself truly blessed and hope you enjoy sharing my journey through the darkness and the light, embracing the many people who have been influential and dear to my journey. I can't thank them enough and I just hope I do them justice when they appear in this drama called life.

...being confident of this, that he who began a good work in you will carry it on to completion until the day of Christ Jesus. - Philippians 1 v 6.

THE EARLY YEARS

I was born bang on the edge of 1964 and spent my first full day alive in Cardiff, Wales, in 1965. It was a very different world then. I owned no photos of myself as a baby or my parents. There was no Facebook or mobile phones to record these daily celebrations of a newborn's beginnings. Cameras and electrical equipment were an extreme luxury and most people didn't own them. I have very little knowledge of the first eighteen months and no memories that I can recall. My father has told me little of my birth mother. In fact, it was only a few years ago that he first showed me a photo of her, and even then, her face was hard to see. Photographs from that era can be small and lack the clarity of today's modern cameras. I discovered that he had 'stolen' me from her in Cardiff Castle's grounds with the aid of my aunty, a story I heard through my first wife, Tina, whom, I can only presume, he must have found easier to tell. I broke down in tears when I heard this. I'm not sure why, to be honest, as I have no complaints about my upbringing, just good memories. I had a roof over my head, clothes on my back, food in my stomach and loving parents, what more could you need? I suppose the sudden tale of my reality came as a shock that split open a wound that had not fully healed, as if a scar had been ripped apart.

I often wonder who I'd be today if he had not done this, if he had left me with my mother. My father is a sensible soul; "everything in moderation" is his motto, something I have always found it hard to adhere to, as I have a different disposition from him (I wonder if that came from my mother). Anyhow, I'm eternally grateful to him for taking me, and I believe my path has been ordained by God. That may sound strange, but a few tales he has told me about his life confirm my belief. For instance, during World War 2, a bomb landed on the roof of his house but did not go off. If it had, I obviously wouldn't be here. Another time, he told me that whilst dating my mother, he had become fed up with paying every time they went out. So, he determined in his mind that if she did not contribute on this one particular night that he would end the relationship with her. Much to his surprise, that evening she footed the whole bill! I said to him, "That was God prompting her dad so that I could be born." He froze and looked at me, puzzled.

At the age of three, I met a new woman who was only a teenager herself. I called her Nita at first, but after a while, I was informed that I should address her as mum, and that is who she has always been. My birth mother has been a 'ghost' and I have rarely given thought to her. Mum was a caring, fussy type, constantly drumming into me how to look, behave and speak, instilling her own moral standard into me from a young age. It has stood me in good stead, but it is not always who I am, and as you will find out, I have rebelled against it for large parts of my life. I do, however, owe so much to the two of them for their love and security. They have been there through thick and thin, protecting me from myself at times, picking me up when I've come crashing down from my destructive side. They have been my earthly rocks.

Whilst I have some fleeting memories of catching a bus to Abercarn with my birth mother to visit my grandparents as a toddler, they remain faceless. I remember goldfish, which my grandfather and I used to catch in a local lake or pond. I would watch horse racing with them and had a bet on the 1971 Derby winner Mill Reef. I was engulfed at a young age by the love of this sport as not only they, but my father and, soon to come, my mother's parents were also fans. Wherever I stayed, whoever I visited, Saturday afternoons were about horse racing. I soon had Totopoly and Escalado, old horse racing games, and it became an obsession of my early years, amusing myself for hours alone with my first great passion. Saturday afternoon horse racing and then football became my only agendas. I loved to watch Match of the Day when I was allowed to stay up late. I had my first Subbuteo set at the age of four or five and remember taking it out to friends' houses to play as well as playing matches and running leagues by myself. I owned a meticulously kept book in which I wrote fixtures and league tables. One of my first friends, whom we called 'Fatty Martin', seems cruel now, but it was a name indicative of the times, called once with his Subbuteo kit under his arms, barely able to carry it. "Can Steve play?" he would ask as if we were about to take it out on the streets!

The streets were relatively safe then, though. As young as five, we would all take a ball over the local parks or down the lanes of Penylan parent-free. There were very few cars on the road and little threat from society. Our ball would inevitably fly over gardens and we would take it in turns to knock on their doors to get it back, oblivious to the nuisance factor. A wonderful life for a kid and so much simpler than the technology-riddled world youngsters find themselves in now. In my quiet moments at home, I became interested in music, listening to the radio and singing along to 'Lily the Pink', 'Puff the Magic Dragon' and other silly tunes of the 1960s until one day I heard 'My Coo Ca Choo' by Alvin Stardust. I became obsessed, spending hours with the radio, desperate for that tune to air. We lived in a downstairs flat below my grandparents, my father's father, and it was his radio I would hog. He also had a small record collection, none of which I can remember, but I loved to flick through it. My father had a love of jazz, which I didn't share. He was a drummer and set his drum kit up in the living room. He would frighten the life out of me with them. I don't know why, but I was petrified of the cymbals. He was also a saxophone player. I began to love music, although jazz made absolutely no sense to me at the time, it was just a noise without lyrics.

At the age of seven and having five or six good friends I played with daily, my parents announced that we were moving to an area called Birchgrove. I remember feeling slightly devastated, but, was reassured that I would still see my old friends. These were, of course, words of comfort, not truth, but they helped, and I was cast into a new area briefly alone. I started at Birchgrove Junior School and soon made new friends. One in particular became an important early influence, Andy. We grew a close friendship which we took together into Whitchurch High School.

He wasn't a fan of horse racing or football, though, so I developed other friendships. Lynn was one who especially loved football and we would spend days in parks and lanes, picking up where I left off with my crew from Penylan. We played golf as well at Heath Park. When it was raining, we would indulge in Subbuteo like it was going out of fashion. Then, in high school, more friendships flowered, and another young lad called Andrew became my main Subbuteo buddy along with Lynn. He had a 'dream come true' set up in his garage with the pitch laid out on a big board, floodlights and all the necessary accessories. We would take regular walks to Whitchurch Road, where there was a shop that sold Subbuteo to buy new teams and soon built a big collection. This naturally led to us starting our own World Cup.

Nations were drawn into groups and matches were played. I remember loving the administration side of it all. The carefully planned organisation and records that needed to be done were a joy for me. It was, looking back, ridiculously ambitious, as we only ever got to the first round or two of matches. There were too many games to be played and, in truth, it may have taken us years to finish it, so the outcome was never reached to my knowledge. These two people especially helped feed my early lust for pleasure.

In the first year of high school, a boy in my class, Rob, came to the fore. He was the first person my age I'd ever met who loved horse racing. Until then, I had only shared this passion with my family, but Rob and I would share a love of that and, briefly, car spotting. My first trip to Chepstow racecourse was with Rob when we were eighteen. It was magical. We caught a train, walked through the town and there, in front of us, was the racecourse rolled out like a giant party invitation for the rest of my life. I had only known this sport as a picture on TV every Saturday, but that day it became a real-life experience. From that point on, we would go as often as we could, later extending our experience to places like Ludlow and Hereford. It was about then that one of my ambitions was born, to visit every racecourse in Britain during my lifetime, so I started ticking them off, one by one, when time and finance allowed.

Sometimes I would go with Rob, sometimes with another fanatic I had met, Alan, and sometimes on my own. I've never really had a problem with doing things I love by myself if a partner in crime could not be found.

Elsewhere in my early to mid-teens, I was given a New Testament and Psalms and being aired on TV was the series Jesus of Nazareth. I watched it with my parents, eagerly awaiting my Sunday instalment.

Something about this man's life grabbed my heart in a way I had never experienced before. At night, I would read His story in the gospels under my bed sheets with a torch (I was supposed to be sleeping). The love and kindness that this man showed people touched my young heart. His words were so wise and profound, and then the punishment that was inflicted upon Him seemed completely and utterly unfair. I felt for Him, I was, to use a modern term, outraged! I read, over and over, the crucifixion story. His words on the cross were incredible to me. "Forgive them Father, for they know not what they do." What? This was amazing, awesome, it gripped me and held me captive. I was not brought up with any kind of religion and didn't really understand it, but something about this man was like nothing else I had encountered. This was my first brief experience of a loving God.

ANARCHY IN THE UK

One day, while visiting Andy, he excitedly took me to his bedroom and said he had heard of this band called the Sex Pistols and needed to play their album to me. Music had always been in the background of my life, I had bought a few records growing up. The first one I had purchased was Seven Seas of Rhye by Queen and I loved Abba. I embraced Grease when it came out, seeing the film in the pictures and buying the album. I would sing along and dance like a fool in my bedroom. None of that prepared me for what I was about to hear.

Neither did I know that I would leave his bedroom on the edge of being a very different person. Pretty Vacant, God Save the Queen, and Anarchy in the UK spilled gratefully into my attentive ears, birthing seeds that were about to become the driving force of my being and thinking. It was around 1979, so the Pistols and the punk rock movement had started impacting Britain's society a few years before, but I had completely missed it. Nevertheless, I was soon turning into a different person, developing a new way of semi-immature thinking which rejected everything my parents had taught me to be and relishing being rebellious, free-thinking and unique. I began rejecting the mainstream "normal" ways and transformed myself quickly into something that horrified my mother. My record collection was growing rapidly, as were the bands I was listening to. In typically 'me' fashion, I became obsessed, and my earlier passions struggled to find a window into my life. Warfare arose in my family as I wanted to dye my hair, wear crazy clothes and 'be myself' to fit in with my new friends who were into the same music but my parents forbade it. So I was limited to scruffy jeans, a leather jacket and a bad attitude towards all authority! I was never able to openly defy my parents. Strangely, my first leather jacket came as a Christmas present from my grandmother. My mother must have been beside herself, her own mother providing the very thing she was trying to stop me from having. I'm sure that in her mind, she must have been disowning me. All she had brought me up to be was rapidly flying out of the window, and she was powerless to stop it. We would argue like never before and not speak to each other for days at a time. I'm sure she dreaded me leaving the house in full view of the neighbours.

Being a punk in those days brought plenty of attention to yourself; we were rejects of society!

I didn't care, though. Reckless abandon flourished as I found this new life, and when the UK Subs came to the Top Rank on 26 October 1980, I was ready for my first gig. I recall being so nervous and yet excited at the prospect of seeing a live band. Walking up Queen Street in Cardiff's city centre towards the venue, I noticed a long line of mainly kids. They had different coloured hair, an array of wacky hairstyles and were clad in their own versions of themselves, like a rainbow of rebellion. I felt an overpowering surge of being part of something that was like nothing I had ever experienced before. I was sold out on it, my life now dedicated to a new cause, singing a new anthem, my soul crying out, "Look at me, I belong!"

I was fifteen and still in school. I had been placed into a new class that term and had a few new faces in front of me. Rob was still in my class, so my passion for horse racing continued to be fed, but my interest had turned more by now, and one of the new faces, little did I know, was about to become my lifelong friend and a major player in my story, Cez. At first, I noticed we would laugh at the same stupid things, enjoy playing childish tricks on each other, and generally getting ourselves in petty trouble with teachers. One in particular, our English teacher, Mrs Duffield, was to be a regular 'victim'. She was a fantastic teacher in hindsight but her proper manners and ways forced silly children like us to push her and take advantage. Most of the kids in our class liked to mess around. We didn't lack intelligence, more the will to use it properly through boring teaching and irrelevant lessons, and so our classmates became our audience in the theatre of stupidity. When someone was called to the front of the class to read, roughly drawn penises were seen appearing below desks, backed up by big smiles on cheeky faces. The rollover blackboard would be decorated with a large penis and hidden, ready to be revealed as the teacher rolled it around to clean. We cared little for maturity, and that was exactly how Mrs Duffield dealt with it, ignoring what was put before her and carrying on dutifully. I have never forgotten some of the things she taught me, even though I failed English. She tried splitting us up to little effect, as we were mostly in it together. She managed an impossible job very well. We were sent to stand outside the door to see the headmaster, but this didn't stop us. That may not seem strange now, but in those days, you could end up being caned or thrashed with a dap (trainer) or rope. It could be painful to disobey the teacher, they demanded respect. Some were brutal. Once, three of us were caught messing around by the French teacher. He lined us up, grabbed the two outside heads and banged them onto the head of the middle kid. Ouch! He probably would be sacked or assaulted in today's schools. Cez and another kid, Nigel, were my main cohorts. We just loved to play the fools and, as a result, eventually left school with far worse grades than we were capable of.

I still played football in school, though. Every break time was taken up kicking a ball around the playground. I had been the top scorer in Junior School for their team, but on arrival at Whitchurch found the rugby biased games; teachers would only allow so many to play football, the rest of us being herded off, like obedient sheep, to play rugby. I hated it and still do. Hence, the relief of playing football during breaks. One friend, another Andrew, who was involved with us, wasn't the best. I would wind him up at times as I saw some of his actions as daft. He refused to take his turn in goals (everyone hated that) and then would have a go at me for not saving a shot. Considering we often played with a tennis ball, I found it harsh and, one day, I blasted the tennis ball at him full pelt, shouting "save this then". The ball caught him square in the face. He stood shocked for a moment before chasing me around the pitch, trying to punch me. I was faster than him, though, so he eventually ran out of breath and will. Another time, in line with our tomfoolery, I took all of his school books out of his bag when he wasn't looking and replaced them with a couple of bricks. This was met with howls of laughter when he stood puzzled back in class. Andrew was in Birchgrove with me, and we were friends on the whole. He had two younger brothers, Simon and Stephen, who will appear later on. Something about Andrew's ways always used to provoke me, though. In maths, we both got into trouble for not doing our homework. Whilst we stood in front of the teacher offering explanations, I lied through my teeth and he broke down crying. It reminded me of Junior school where, at the age of eight, we were made to stand up and recite our 3 times table. When it was his turn, he was unable to do it and blamed me for 'putting him off'. Characters like him still played their part, though and I don't want ridicule for him as we all have our foolish ways.

The really important things in my mind were happening outside of school. As part of my need to be part of the music, I bought an electric guitar but quickly gave up as I couldn't make my fingers obey the chord structures, so I replaced it, on Nigel's advice, with a bass guitar. It seemed like everyone was buying some kind of instrument, it was part of being punk. Cez had a drum kit in his garage, as did Andy. The dream became to be in a band, and a few, including Cez and Snappy, started one in Cez's garage. Snappy was the singer. I had known him for most of my life, off and on, he was arguably my oldest friend. It turned out that he lived in the same street as Cez and was also a punk. I'd known him as Gareth, but under the new regime, he'd been labelled Snappy because he was thin. He would join me, Andy and Cez in our quest for adventure. Somehow, one typically foolish night, we started calling each other 'John'. It stuck like glue, and we have been affectionately doing it ever since. My school nickname was Stef, so I had now developed three names, Steve, Stef and John, depending on my location and company.

The four of us would stroll up to Rhiwbina village most nights, where we would meet up with other like-minded youngsters. Vaughan, Jayne and her sister Helen, Sarah and Rob, who lived in the village but were more of a Queen fan. There were others who would come and go on certain nights, but this was our gang. We would meet at a bench in the village pretty much every night, probably making passersby very nervous. It was on one of those nights that I learnt to smoke. I coughed my guts up at first, but stuck at it as it seemed 'cool' and was another part of my 'fitting in' process. Like everyone, I had to work hard to become addicted, but after buying a couple of packets, I became a fully fledged smoker, although I learned to hide it skillfully from my parents. I think my father had an inkling, as he was a smoker himself. I would stuff tissue in my box of matches so that they didn't rattle in my leather jacket when I took it off at home. It would be something I would become quite professional at, hiding stuff from my parents. One night, whilst sitting on the bench, a friend of the family walked by, saw me smoking and smiled. She must have gone straight home and phoned my parents to tell them. On returning that evening, I had to face an interrogation, but unashamedly lied through my teeth to get out of it, another defence mechanism I developed to cover my ever-increasing rebellious lifestyle. A few of us also went to the Beulah Youth Club in the village.

Andy, "The Beulah Youth Club days! We went on a camping trip with them to the West Country. I remember us sneaking out to the local pub and buying a couple of bottles of cider. On the way out, we bumped into the leaders and they confiscated it!"

The next powerful influence on me occurred when Rob arrived one evening with what he called 'bush'. It was a peculiar little package consisting of twigs, leaves and seeds. Clumsily, he showed us how to construct a joint, sticking three rizlas together, splitting open a cigarette and sprinkling the aforementioned substance on top before rolling it and carefully placing a rolled bit of cardboard in one end. He lit it, took a few puffs and passed it to me. The effects took me to a place I never knew existed, and naively, I fell in love with it. Shortly after, Snappy took me to the house of a fellow punk called Stein. He was, to me, a fully fledged marijuana smoker, and I sat in his dining room with him, Snappy and a couple of other strangers being introduced to a bong and chillums. Steve Miller's 'The Joker' was playing as I watched Stein make a 'mull'. A few 'tokes' later, Steve Miller was singing 'Fly like an Eagle' and that is exactly what I was doing in my mind. My love of marijuana was well and truly born.

So here was my new life, music, gigs, marijuana and pleasure at all costs. I started having no regard for what I was putting in my body, which led to alcohol, a couple of acid trips, magic mushrooms and speed or amphetamines. I wanted pleasure at all costs. I had an amazing new set of friends, was learning to play bass guitar along to records in my bedroom, getting smashed out of my mind and generally not caring about anything as I was about to leave school.

Then, shortly before my final exams started, my mother told me that I had to stay in to revise. Not disastrous under normal circumstances but what she really meant was I couldn't go out at all for the next month or so. Lockdown! This was a short period of my life that would send me over the edge. Whilst my friends were out, I was in. Even weekends! The only time I was allowed out of the house was to go to school, and when I did, my behaviour became more rebellious. I had to let off steam, and my teachers took the brunt of it. I would refuse to do homework, telling one teacher, in my ignorance, that it was because I had run away from home. To my great surprise and my mother's horror, Social Workers knocked on the door that evening to investigate my 'disappearance'. My anthem became Stiff Little Fingers' 'At the Edge', blasting out in my bedroom, the justifiably comforting lyrics, "And I'm running at the edge of their world, they're criticising something they just can't understand, living on the edge of their town, and I won't be shot down." I invented games, read anything bar school work and hid it all when I heard someone coming upstairs, pretending to revise. I cried, made charts counting the days to my release and devised any means of pleasure I could think of to get through the experience. By the time it was over, I was damaged mentally.

Nobody was ever going to tell me what to do again in my life. I was determined to make up for lost time and wreak my own sense of anarchy in the UK! I achieved 3 'O' Levels as they were known, French, Maths and Technical Drawing. This was way short of what I was probably capable of, but I didn't care. I just wanted out of the hell known as school.

In the background of all this, I had developed an interest in the occult. I'd taken part in a few Ouija board sessions at a friend's house. It seemed real as the glass moved over our homemade board spelling out people's names. I wondered and hoped that none of the participants were pushing the glass. I distinctly remember one girl, Janine, who was wearing a cross, having to leave the room as ordered by the board. We told a few other tales, like saying the Lord's Prayer backwards in a mirror would summon the devil to appear behind you and feeling thrilled, nervous and excited all rolled into one. No one tried that, to my knowledge. I was taking it all very seriously, considering my naturally childish approach to most other things, and when a few kids started messing around, I went into the other room and refused to get involved. A few minutes later, I heard a crash, and they all piled out of the room in haste, screaming as if being chased by the forces of darkness themselves. A book had flown onto the piano independently and frightened the life out of them. This just confirmed my suspicions that it was something very real. Shortly after, I went out and bought a pack of Tarot Cards and a book on how they worked. When I got familiar with them, I was offering to do readings for my friends. I predicted the death of a cat and other trivial things, but I became aware that they had an unexplainable power. I carried them with me quite often, feeling they gave me some kind of status and on a visit to Jayne and Helen's one day, I read them to their father. I didn't know him, but told him he spent time in courtrooms to which he was astonished, as that was a big part of his job. I'd hit the nail on the head but again, nothing major. The biggest one was on its way.

SCHOOL'S OUT

And out I came. My parents gave me a choice of staying in school or getting a job. Whilst a few of my mates had left and signed on, that was not an option. I had no idea what I wanted to do with my life, what career path to take, so I ended up in a factory on a six-month Youth Opportunity Programme, a government-backed initiative to find youngsters permanent employment. The pay was £25 a week, which seemed a fortune. I gave my mother £10, saved £5 and was left with £10 to spend on mainly vices. I flourished there, RHS Engineering. The owner was an older gentleman, Roy, who treated me well, and the foreman was also very accommodating. He would say, "Up here for thinking, down there for dancing" as he pointed to his head and feet. It was a small factory with about 15 employees, a kind of family set-up. They all welcomed me, and I gained valuable work experience in the various aspects of factory life, a fine introduction to my work education. After my six-month term ended there, I was summoned to Roy's office, where he regretfully told me he couldn't keep me on, even though he was impressed by my work and attitude.

So I joined another YOP scheme, this time at a larger factory in Llanishen called Aeroquip. Lo and behold, starting at the same time as me was my old schoolmate Rob. For the next eight years of my life, I worked there. I never saw it as my long-term career but as a means to the finance that I needed to fund my pleasure. I had to clock in by 8.00 am every day, which was a nightmare as every night I would be out 'partying'. My mother, eager that I should maintain a good attitude toward work, dutifully took it upon herself to nag me out of bed every morning. She desperately wanted to keep me working. I would typically go to bed after midnight and can only imagine what she went through trying to wake me, probably calling upwards of ten times before I aroused. I grew to hate the sound of my own name being cast into the air. "Steve, come on Steve." I had invested in a push bike and would cycle to work. I had it down to a fine art, arising at 7.45 am, quick swill of my face, on my push bike and in work by 8.00 am. I grew to hate it, that morning drill, feeling exhausted and groggy for the first hour of each day. Coffee was vital once I arrived at work and for the large part, I longed for break time when I would play cards with some colleagues. After a few years there, I was promoted to a lab where I worked on my own. I'd buy the paper on the way in and spend most of the day studying horse racing whilst the machine I had to operate did the work. I read books on gambling and was slowly becoming obsessed again. Rob fuelled the fire and we had a weekly tipster competition between ourselves. So work by day, party by night.

Going back, my first position at the Aeroquip factory was in the storeroom working with a man called Brian. He was a 'valley's boy' and would take the mickey out of my taste in music and general thoughts on life. Saying that, we got on well, and one day, when I told him I was reading the tarot, he insisted that I lay the cards out for him and give him a reading. I refused at first, but due to his persistence, I did, but not without warning him of the dangers. So I proceeded to 'look into his future'. "I see some kind of accident," I told him, clueless as to what that meant. The next day, on arriving at work, he started chasing me around the store, cursing me. He had crashed his car around a lamp post on the way home that night and somehow thought it was my fault. He escaped uninjured, thankfully, but the reality of the occult was becoming stronger in my life.

Outside of work, quite a few of my friends were on the dole (claiming benefits) and seemed to spend days and weeks 'on tour' following bands around the country. I would join them, wherever they were on weekends. London was becoming the place to go. Friday night from work, I'd be on a train and head straight for Brixton, where a guy we had met called Midge lived and used to sleep on the floor at his flat. He was very accommodating. The first time I met him was at a Death Cult gig in London. He walked over, sat opposite me and then flung himself backwards off the chair. Nutcase! I instantly loved him. He was a lovely guy, he smoked pure marijuana in a pipe as he didn't like tobacco and was arguably the best bass player I've ever met. I'd learned to play with a plectrum, but Midge once posed the question, "Why use that little bit of plastic when you have a whole hand to play with?" It made sense, but would mean learning to play all over again and I didn't have the patience at that time.

Myself, Cez, Andy and a couple of others from Cardiff would spend weekends at Midge's, including my old school buddy's brother Simon, who had taken to the lifestyle by now.

I was living the dream as I saw it. We were young, wild and carefree, living the life of, as Ian Dury put it, Sex and Drugs and Rock'n'Roll. We were meeting new like-minded people from all over the country who were following the post punk bands around and often found a place to stay wherever we went. I say 'often' here because it wasn't always the case. We often went to gigs in a town called Aylesbury, which was a terrible place to get out of after a gig.

The last train had always left before the ending, so we used to stroll back to the small train depot, hop onto an empty carriage and sleep in it. One time, Andy, Cez and I woke up on a moving train which was full of commuters. A bizarre experience and strange in a way that the guard hadn't found us. Cez and I hitched back from Aylesbury to London once and spent a few hours in the freezing cold by the roadside. It seemed like no one was going to stop for us, and our limbs were becoming stiff, even wrapped in sleeping bags. Then a man stopped and we jumped into his car, our ticket to London. We talked gratefully with our host all the way back and when Cez jumped out before me as we were going to different places, the guy started talking to me about Jesus Christ. I saw no relevance to it and told him that he should have mentioned it when Cez was in the car, as it was 'his type of thing' (Cez was brought up in a Christian household).

Another time in some place around London, which we couldn't leave, Cez and I slept beside a railway track with some guy we'd met at the gig who was from Liverpool. My ears were ringing from the loud music, and I had trouble understanding him. We slept in our sleeping bags (an essential part of the tour kit) and, on waking, we found ourselves soaking wet and covered in insects. The folly of youth! Seeing the bands was paramount, everything else was secondary. I had no sense of fear, just adventure. A couple of older punks, Beva and Sian, who were from

Pontypridd, had a car and would sometimes take a few of us in the back at a price. I remember them leaving early one Friday afternoon with Andy to go and see a band called Play Dead in Liverpool University. I'd arranged to meet them at the gig as I couldn't leave work until 4.00 pm and was going to catch a lift to Sheffield to see the band the next night. So I hopped on a train after work, arrived at Lime Street train station about 8.00 pm, which was perfect timing. I jumped in the nearest cab and asked for Liverpool University. "Which one?" asked the driver. "How many are there?" I responded. "About eleven!" was his answer. I hadn't planned for this. Remember, there were no mobile phones. I jumped from the cab and strolled around Liverpool town aimlessly, trying to be resourceful when I saw a girl with spiky hair. I ran over and asked if she knew where the gig was, but she didn't. However, she took me to a club where one of the doormen had the answer. Fifteen minutes later, about 9.30, I breathed a huge sigh of relief as I walked into the hall with Play Dead kicking off their set and the smiling faces of Beva, Sian and Andy greeting me. On a Bauhaus tour, Andy and I had nowhere to stay after seeing them in Derby, so we walked through the night to Stoke, where they were playing the next evening. We trudged over mountains and down roads, occasionally stopping to consult our map (another sometimes crucial part of a tour kit) and trying to thumb down the odd car that passed us. We arrived in Stoke at dawn, exhausted and slept on benches in a bus depot.

There are so many other stories like this, but you get the picture. Music was the main driving force for us. Gigs were a do-or-die business by which we gave little regard to safety and lived to be part of the music industry itself. Our group of mates was strong, especially in Cardiff. At gigs, we dominated what is now called the mosh pit. I came to a full realisation of that when I followed New Model Army around on one of their first tours. I went to see them on my own, apart from the odd gig where I managed to talk someone into coming with me. I watched from the side with my Sony Walkman, taping the gig, as their 'followers' dominated the crowd. But then they came to Cardiff and found themselves unable to even dance as 'the crew' pushed them out of the way. It was a great feeling to be part of something so intense. We were like a big family, all looking out for one another. This group had been formed in a pub called the Lexington. It was on Queen Street in Cardiff town centre where the Capitol Centre now stands.

Andy, Cez, Snappy, I and a few others graduated from the streets of Rhiwbina when we were about seventeen. On the weekends we weren't away, we would spend Friday nights in the 'Lex'. Saturday nights too, but with the addition of going on to Neros, a nightclub on Park Place that played our kind of music. Many friends were made in Lexington. It was a small place, downstairs from a delicious burger joint. We could put our own records in the jukebox, and it had a Space Invaders table, which was relatively new at the time. The whole pub knew each other, which was particularly borne out on rugby days. Often, a few rugby fans would stray in on international match days, but the Welsh and English, though, were the problem. They wouldn't be able to resist picking on someone who looked a bit different, only to find the whole pub turn on them and kick them out. The sense of belonging became stronger as did the desire to get smashed. We would have bongs before going to town, travelling on the bus carrying paranoia and were wrecked before the night had begun properly, as many pints as could be afforded in the pub and anything else that was going around, often walking home at 2.00 am 'speeding' only to finish the night smoking weed when we got back. The main question was usually where we could go at that time of the morning to do this. Simon's parents had a catering business, a big house opposite the Monico cinema, and in the back garden was a big hut for the staff. We'd pile in there drunkenly, smoke a pipe or bong, whatever we had and usually end up vomiting. This became our way of life for years in many different places. And Cez would find a safe place to throw up, laughing all the while, and swear we wouldn't do it next week. We always did, though. One particular night that stands strong in my memory, a few of us went back in the early hours to Cez's parents' garage. We got stoned and were messing around when the light went on in the kitchen. His father came out to see what was going on. So, in a panic, we all picked up dumbbells and pretended to be weightlifting. As if!

Andy, *"We invented 'Nutter's Express' with the slogan 'Don't leave home without it'. It was a statement stolen from American Express about what it took to be part of our gang.*

Another night that highlighted the ridiculousness of this, Cez and I had been to town and talked two girls into coming back to our mates' house, Monk. Andy and I had met Monk at the end of our school life. He was the first person I knew of our age who had a car, and his parents had a swimming pool in their garden. Selfishly, we were drawn to him for those reasons. We soon had him smoking weed with us, though, and we became good friends. Anyhow, back we went to Monk's (his parents were away) at 2.00 am, made a mull and minutes later, I staggered to the bathroom with Cez and joined him vomiting, me over the toilet and Cez over the sink. The girls were abandoned, we were wrapped around the bathroom fixtures, and Monk was left with them, not knowing what to do. Needless to say, they were gone when we woke the next day.

Tales like this were many, and everything else, like work and family, was an irrelevant side duty. We lived for thrills and craved them with a passion.

GROWING UP!

It was 1983, I was eighteen and had made up my mind that I was ready to move out and find myself a flat. It was a romantic idea of independence which I hadn't really thought through properly, but with a few friends doing it, and plenty of talk in our circles about it, I started looking. We found a house for rent in Ruby Street, so Andy and I put the word out as we needed four people. A couple of kids we had met at the Lex came forward, Gareth, a budding actor from Caerphilly and Ant, drummer of a local psychobilly band, Demented Are Go. We had our four and took the opportunity with eager anticipation. On breaking the news to my parents, my mother broke down and did her utmost to discourage me. She knew I wasn't ready, but, as I told her, "I'm eighteen and there's nothing you can do." She didn't speak to me during most of this time. Even when I visited, she would turn her back in disgust, heartbreak and despair. I recall being given the key, which wasn't just a means to open the front door but a symbol of freedom and maturity, which I was desperately lacking.

There had been a comedy on TV not long before this called 'The Young Ones' starring Rik Mayall and Ade Edmondson about a bunch of students living in poverty and filth. Ruby Street was close to echoing that, if not worse in some ways. It was one long party. My eating habits, having to fend for myself, collapsed as most of my meals came from the local chip shop on Clifton Street. The neighbours were thrown headlong into torment as music blasted out through the night. Drugs were rife, and I struggled to know the difference between night and day. I called work frequently pretending to be sick, stretching my luck and their patience. I was never really ill, but desperate to maintain the life of a practising hedonist. The place was always full of visitors as it became the focal point of the friends we all had, and quickly became a den of iniquity. We all dropped acid one night, and when 'the trip' kicked in, Andy and Ant vanished, locking themselves into their bedrooms. So with just Gareth and me left, we embarked on a great adventure, developing the idea that we were judges out of Judge Dredd. I don't remember too much of that night, but one instant that sticks out was the pair of us venturing out the front door about 6.00 am to get some milk and Gareth crushing an ant, proclaiming, "He's been judged!" We all had girlfriends at the time, and mine, my first proper one as I saw it, Beccy, tried hard to help me. She brought me tinned food and bought me a bean bag for my room. It was a lovely gesture, and she nobly stuck with me through this short period. I can't imagine how she viewed it, as she was far more sensible than I ever was. Months later, and to highlight my immaturity at the time, I dumped her by inviting her to my house and ignoring her for hours until she eventually went home. I felt terrible about that years later, but we live and learn.

It was a matter of a mere two months until, in poor health and on the verge of being sacked, I returned home like the Prodigal Son. My parents welcomed me with open arms and duly put me back on track. I'd still visit Ruby Street some nights, but the whole experience had taught me the limits of my frailties, and I gave no thought to moving out for quite a few years after.

We started to develop a new, local scene. The brothers, Simon and Stephen, were not getting on very well, so their parents put a caravan in their drive for Simon to live in. A new focal point of nightly entertainment. We would meet there most nights to get stoned or drunk if we couldn't score weed. We would listen to music and play cards. I, Cez, Simon, Rob, Monk and Andy were the main residents. Simon's father was a well-built, intimidating chap who hated marijuana, so we had to be careful when he was around. I heard of one occasion when he knocked on the door, burst into the caravan and proceeded to punch the living daylights out of Simon. Andy slipped quietly and quickly out, but Monk was stuck behind Simon, trying to avoid the onslaught. I had fortunately left about five minutes before this happened and received the story the night after with great amusement. These were fond memories as the caravan gave us a relatively safe place to go, away from the streets and our parents' glare. Alongside this, Stephen was nurturing his love of smoking weed with a school friend, Peter, who later became known as Pedro. They weren't allowed into our scene, though, as they were seen as youngsters who didn't have a clue. Besides, Simon had no intention of allowing his brother to interfere or acquaint himself with his circle.

Simon, regarding the beating from his father, "We all hitchhiked to a party in Newbury the week before. I was the only person who made it and had the sides of my head shaved into a mohican. It was a red flag moment for my dad and a couple of days later, he kicked off as was the way back then."

I had a very frightening and powerful experience somewhere around this time. I was walking home stoned from Simon's one evening down Pantbach Road in the dark, thinking to myself about the history of the area. I wondered what it looked like hundreds of years ago, plain fields perhaps. For some reason, a strong sense of paranoia came over me, and I began to hear a strange voice in my head. Minutes later, standing at the front door of my house, this voice told me, "I'm going to set your mother on you." As I turned the key and entered, my mother came rushing out of the living room. "What's wrong? You don't look well," she asked. I didn't feel well, the voice laughed, tormenting me, so I made a quick excuse and ran to the safety of my bedroom. I jumped into bed and wrestled with my sanity. My mother came in to see what was happening, and I yelled at her to leave me. The voice told me it was going to take my mind and led me down a bricked hallway, the type you see in a castle. At the end was a door with a sign saying, 'DO NOT OPEN.' I couldn't stop myself from opening it, and all kinds of madness came pouring out into my head. I lay there paralysed, thinking I was about to lose my mind to an evil force and mercifully must have fallen asleep. I didn't smoke weed for about a month after that creepy encounter with darkness. I remember talking to Midge about it, and he told me he'd had a similar experience and couldn't smoke for a while either.

My first glimpse into the world of 'celebrity' came in 1986. Gareth had left for London after Ruby Street and starred in a TV drama called 'The District Nurse' in 1984 with Nerys Hughes. He went on to land a six-month contract in EastEnders as Ian Beale's band manager. I met up with him whenever I was in London and soon became aware that wherever we went, we were being followed, mainly by teenage girls pointing and giggling. He would be approached for his signature or by the star-struck brigade constantly and described it recently to me as the 'worst period of his life'. It's easy to understand what he meant. One evening whilst in London, I went with Gareth and Andy for a few pints and, a few hours later, we stumbled from the pub looking for somewhere to eat. We entered a Pizza Hut, took a table and dashed over to the salad bar for some instant satisfaction. In our haste and condition, we were piling salad onto their large laminated menus and carting it back to the table to scoff when a waitress stormed over, fully intent on telling us off or even throwing us out. She took one look at Gareth and froze, adopting a completely different attitude and soon forgetting her original purpose. As Gareth's character was quite controversial, he suffered a bad experience at the hands of people who failed to separate TV and reality. He was beaten up and appeared in the daily newspaper with a couple of black eyes.

In town around this time, The Lexington had shut down, and our scene had moved to the upstairs floor of The Model Inn. New people emerged all the time, and I noticed a couple of girls with bleached hair I'd never seen before. They didn't seem to be mixing with anyone else and rumours were going around that they were lesbians. One drunken evening, I plucked up the courage to speak to them and they introduced themselves as Justine and Esther. They were from Llantrisant way and didn't know many people in Cardiff. I stared at Justine, thinking to myself she was the most beautiful girl I'd ever seen and, as the weeks went by, I would look out for them. In conversation one night, Justine suggested that I accompany her back to her place after closing hours. I thought she was joking, "What about your parents?" I asked her. "They are quite liberal and don't mind boys sleeping on my bedroom floor." I'd somehow hit the jackpot in my eyes. We caught the last bus back to Llantrisant, got off at Talbot Green and walked a mile or so to her house in Pontyclun. I was overwhelmed that such a beauty was taking me back to her house and, at the same time, nervous in case she was lying about her parents. On arrival, the house was quiet. We sat on the sofa in her living room, talking, and then she kissed me. I instantly and helplessly fell in love for the first time in my life. No disrespect to my previous short flings, but something about this girl made me melt. I felt like I would do anything for her. Our relationship was distant for the first six months. Due to the distance between us, I only saw her at The Model Inn on a Friday or Saturday. We rarely rang each other in the week and often would ignore each other on arrival at the pub. It was as if neither wanted to make the first move to say hello, like a game of love chess. I would think about her all the time, and once, while walking with Snappy one day said to him, "I've never been so in love. I can't and don't even look at any other girls."

I was 21 by now and, being a few years younger than me, she was doing her end-of-school exams so hadn't been around for a couple of weeks. Out of the blue, I had a letter. It was from her, and to this day I wish I had kept it. She opened up to me, saying she missed me and had strong feelings for me. I was like a mould of jelly, wobbling, weak-kneed and besmitten. Shortly after, I caught a bus to her house, and we sat in her bedroom expressing our love for each other. "No matter where I go, what I do with my life, I'll never forget you," she told me. I wanted to marry her, but she rejected my proposal as she had ideas of travelling to France and spending time there. Her French was good, and she spoke fondly of wanting to live there. My heart broke when she told me these things, as I really didn't like the idea myself.

We were much closer now and would spend more time together or speaking on the phone. I remember being in a friend's house, weight training one summer evening, when a mate turned up saying Justine was looking for me. "What do you mean?" I asked. "She's come down to find you, and your parents told her you were out." I knew where to find her as she only knew where Simon lived in Cardiff, so I ran there immediately, heart skipping. Then, as the year came to a close, she told me she was going to France for a while and that our relationship was over. I took her to town, cheque book in hand, and bought her a ring to remember me by. We cried, and I felt my heart was broken. My disposition was one of great sadness for weeks after, and shockingly to me, on a night out, she turned up with one of the goths. I pulled her onto the dance floor and asked her what she was playing at, but her answer made no sense to me. I threatened the goth she was with, which wasn't my style. I've never been a fighter, but our gang and the goths weren't the best of friends anyway, even though we moved in the same clubs and circles. I saw her walk home with him that night and consoled myself by getting smashed. Not long after, around Christmas, we were having a party at Simon's and she turned up. My heart skipped a beat, and we talked and talked like the oldest of friends. She came back to my place that night (my parents were away). In the morning, she left, and that was the last time I saw her. For the next seven years, apart from the odd fling, I failed miserably with girls.

Meanwhile, Andy had met a new girlfriend who was from California, called Brenda. He had met her in London, and one day he told me that he was going over to California with her. I recall waving goodbye to him in Birchgrove and saying, "I'll see you soon." He was one of my best and closest mates at this time, and I thought he wouldn't be gone for long. I was quite used to friends shooting off for a few weeks on tour, so I took it as the norm. What I didn't know was that he would, to date, never come back to this country to live. He came back for a couple of months a year later, but I think I've seen him four or five times since. You never know when the last time you will see someone is!

I flew to California to stay with him a year later on my own. The savings I had been putting away since I started work were enough to pay for a month's stay with him. The credit for this has to go to the wisdom of my mother, who made me save. He was about to marry Brenda and had asked me to be his best man. Halfway through my stay, his sister and his parents turned up. I'd known them a long time and his sister, James, became a good friend. Her name was Alison but for some reason Andy had always called her James. That was an amazing experience, and a few years later, in 1989, I went back there with Monk. The most memorable thing was travelling to the valleys, as it was called, to a reggae festival in Humboldt County. We had hired a car as Monk could drive and had a large bag of marijuana with us. I was rolling a couple of spliffs whilst travelling down the highway when a police car appeared behind us with its sirens blaring and flagging for us to pull over. To say we panicked is an understatement! Monk jumped out of the car, which was a bad idea, whilst I desperately hid the stuff under the car seat. We had been speeding, and fortunately, after realising we were British, they gave Monk a lecture about staying in the car and a court summons. It could have been so much worse, but we arrived in one piece. Strolling along this beautiful place, sun blasting out, we saw a rastafarian coming towards us. "Nice day", Monk said to him and I burst out laughing. When is it not a nice day in California? We saw The Wailers at that festival, and I was beginning to become a big fan of Bob Marley and reggae.

Anyway, back home, I had another 'funny' experience occur somewhere in all this. I was walking into town from Canton to catch the last bus one night when a complete stranger stopped me and said, "God has asked me to speak to you." I don't remember a word he said, but sat on the bus home thinking it was a little crazy. Why on earth would anyone stop me at that time of night, claiming to have words from God? I soon gave no further thought to the experience, but have never forgotten it.

MUSIC MAKES THE WORLD GO AROUND

I was in my first band when I was sixteen. Me, Cez and Beano had a couple of rehearsals in a room in Calvary Baptist Church in Canton. Finding practice space wasn't easy, as it cost money, which we didn't have, and we made plenty of noise. Cez's parents were Christians, so his father pulled the strings for that to happen. Cez was on drums, I was playing bass, and Beano played guitar. We were pretty terrible but didn't care; we were learning our trade and that was the punk ethos. Buy an instrument, form a band and see what happens. Beano was from Cilfynydd near Pontypridd and a couple of years younger than us. I don't remember how we met him, but he was 'a wild one'. If a fight broke out, Beano was your man, he seemed fearless and was only around the scene for a couple of years, then we heard he had assaulted a policeman, and half of Wales's police force was looking for him. Next, I heard that he had joined the army only to go AWOL. Then I heard nothing about him for years.

A few years on, and Cez joined up with some other guys, Mark (guitarist), another Mark (drummer) and Peter (bass). They were better and their songs were quite mature for the time. I jumped in with some vocals occasionally and would go to most of their weekly practices at The Maltings in Splott. They did a couple of gigs in town, as far as I remember and then Peter quit for some reason, leaving a space for me to jump in. I think it was a while after and we moved to some rooms down the back of town, behind Jacob's Market. We were loud, amps up full blast and ears taking a pounding. Our drummer recalled that the door opened during one practice, and one of the Manic Street Preachers told us to "turn it down." Not sure if that is true, but it's always amused me. We played about eight gigs, the highlight being the support act for the UK Subs in the Welsh Club, and made a demo and then broke up. Can't even remember why.

Cez and I continued to write songs and started a new band with our friend Malfy on drums. We'd met him in the Great Western, which is where we had gone after the Model Inn lost our interest. Again, though, apart from a tape recording of a practice, we had nothing to show.

Still, we wrote and after a while, Cez and I packed in the idea of finding a drummer, and we did a few gigs on our own. We weren't after success, we just loved to play music. Cez had moved into a house with Monk during all this but that didn't last long. Monk had bought a house in Splott, his hand forced by his father, who owned properties himself. Pedro moved in with Monk, but that didn't last long either. Cez had moved around the corner into a house with Cam. We met Cam in the Great Western. I remember the first time I saw her. Buoyant black hair, black top, black trousers and white socks above black shoes. Something stood out but I was too nervous to speak to her for a long time. I got to know her well one night in the Poets Corner, a pub on City Road. She sat next to me and we talked. I remember her saying, "I look at you and don't see a double aura as I do with most people." I took that as a compliment and we became good friends.

Cez remembers, "Towards the end of my stay at Monk's, I was getting desperate for some answers to life. I was drinking and smoking heavily and one night in particular got wrecked and proceeded to burn sentimental gifts from my ex-girlfriend in the garden. Monk came out to check if I was alright and I flung unmerited abuse at him. In fairness, he was only looking out for me."

One very memorable night at Cam and Cez's, we were having a party, surprise, surprise. Midge was down from London and we were sitting in the bedroom, wrecked, egging him on to play bass for us. He turned on the amp and proceeded to enthral and entertain us at one o'clock in the morning. The guy was a joy to watch, and I could only dream of being as good as he was. Within minutes, the bedroom door flew open and a red-faced neighbour started hurling abuse at us, basically telling us to shut it down. He left and we did but not without a few giggles. I've since experienced this from the other side, if you like and can see what inconsiderate idiots we were, but at the time it was just rock'n'roll.

Back at work, I'd now spent eight years of my life in a factory and was beginning to get really bored with it. I needed a bigger challenge and was ready for one. I was listening to The Clash's Sandinista album, and one of the tracks, The Magnificent Seven, seemed to be talking to me. "Ring, ring, seven am, move yourself to go again. Cold water in the face brings you back to this awful place." Their lyrics rang true in my life. I'd never considered it before but I started looking in the paper for a new job. It was there that I noticed William Hill, the bookmaker, were hiring. So I applied and was appointed for an interview and, after a short maths test, given a cashier's job. When I told Rob, he was devastated and did his best to discourage me. We had worked together from school practically and he was far more cautious than me. He was telling me I was foolish to leave, but my mind was made up. My first day was in their branch in Pantmawr, and I started at eleven o'clock. I walked into the shop, was shown behind the counter and taken through some basic training. I remember thinking to myself, 'somebody is actually going to pay me to stand in a bookie's all day and watch racing. Have I arrived in heaven? I thought to myself then that I would never take a job I didn't enjoy ever again.

Memorably, one morning, I was about to leave for work and was alone in the house as my parents had both left earlier for their jobs when the doorbell rang. I answered and an old man was standing there. He spoke to me for a short time about Jesus. I listened, frozen and glued to his words with a sense of peace flowing over me. He finished, I shut the door and ran around the back to leave as I was running a little late. Twenty seconds later, I was out the front and couldn't see him anywhere. It seemed impossible as we had a long enough drive for him to not have walked out of sight. I checked both neighbours just in case he'd run, which was unlikely, but nothing. It was as if he'd vanished into thin air.

Much of my social scene had moved to Splott by the age of twenty-four and I no longer had the problem of having to get up early for work. Monk had a vacancy at his place and I discussed the possibility of moving in with him. After his bad experiences with previous friends as tenants, he was reluctant, but I promised to be good and not upset him. It felt right moving out this time, and although my parents were upset to see me go, they knew I was in a different place than the first attempt. Life was taking an amazing new turn. I felt so free and philosophical. I had been developing a new love for music, Bob Marley. I bought quite a few of his albums and had them pumping out in my bedroom, as Monk wasn't a fan. Some of his lyrics spoke to me of a life I wanted to live. I'd spend a few evenings around Cam's who lived around the corner, discussing life, and she became a close friend. Monk worked in a cinema in town, so would come home late from work, and we'd smoke weed together. The social scene had moved more to The Claude, a pub in Roath, where I'd play pool with Malfy.

We had regular card nights at Monks. Life was good, but I had begun to question many things. I was particularly troubled by some of the arguments and discord between my mates. On the way home from my parents' one Sunday evening, I stopped in town for a couple of pints by myself and wrote about four pages on why, when life is so good, do people have to hate each other and other questions that were troubling me at the time. I must have been 'getting things off my chest' to myself!

My career at William Hill had taken off. With a superior knowledge of horse racing to most, if not all employees, I got noticed by my boss, Bernard. After nine months as a cashier, I became a manager. I was excelling within the company, working on relief in Cardiff and Barry and it looked like the sky was the limit. I had found my niche in life, or so I thought. I ran my own competitions through all the shops in Cardiff, and everyone in the company knew me and often requested to have me work with them. I invented a new bet and sent my idea to the marketing department in Leeds but heard nothing. About a month later, I walked into a rival company's shop, Coral, and there was my idea proudly displayed on their screen. I couldn't believe it and, outraged, I wrote to the Managing Director. Word came back down the management line and I was given a position on their regional marketing committee. This was actually quite boring and not what I was interested in but it seemed like another stepping stone.

I'd now been at Monk's for close to three years, and whilst happy there, a flat had become available above one of William Hill's shops in Penylan Road. It was a big place, three stories, and the rent was a mere £40 a week. Things were about to change.

DAWNING OF A NEW ERA

As content as I was at Monk's, getting my own place made sense at that time. Monk was actually upset. "Everyone else I've been happy to see the back of, but I don't want you to leave," he told me. We had very little in common apart from our love of marijuana and playing cards. We were close friends, though, but the time was right and the offer was too good to turn down. I approached Cez about moving in with me, and he took it up. On the ground floor, there was a room we used for practising, which led to a kitchen of sorts. No hot water, but it had a sink. On the first floor was a spare room, bathroom, again no hot water and our massive living room. There was no heating, so we bought a Calor Gas Heater. The second floor held two attic rooms, which we took as our bedrooms. We loved it and would spend hours jamming and having friends around to get wrecked. I would stay up much later than Cez as our work commitments were a little different, and one night, whilst sitting in my bedroom, I heard Cez get up and trundle downstairs to the toilet. Being a bit of a joker, I crept into his room and hid behind the door on my hands and knees. I waited for what seemed like ages, there were no lights on, and then I heard him coming back upstairs. I was bursting to laugh, but restrained it, and as he entered sleepily back into the room, I ran my fingers over his feet, making a frantic squeaking noise. He leapt backwards, squealing like an old woman while I rolled around the floor, finally able to let out my hysterics. After cursing me out, we went back to bed, where I giggled like my old schoolboy self for about an hour afterwards. I could occasionally hear Cez laughing in the other room.

Then one Sunday evening Cez came back from church and we went for a pint in The Claude. He used to go on some Sundays to placate his parents, but had no real interest. He had given his life to God as a young lad, but turned away from that life in school and rarely talked about it. He told me that night over a pint that he had had enough of the world and was 'going back to his faith'. I said I was happy for him, even though I had no idea what that meant. He started to change over the next few days; he stopped smoking marijuana for one, which I found strange and other little changes. He would speak to me about his new faith, and I would debate the relevance of it with my own developing philosophical ideas. Then he said something that made my mind ponder over and over. "Why do you think people use the name of Jesus Christ as a swear word?" Good point! I had no idea but knew that it was something I and others did on a daily basis. I dwelt on this and a few other things until one night, in the early hours of the morning, I was sitting on my own and picked up a tract that he had given me to read. The words seemed to have some sort of life. They sprang off the page and were pouring with great meaning into my heart. I said aloud, "God, if you are real, show me", and felt a loving, powerful force flow through my body. I left a message for Cez outside his room that night, telling him what had happened. I could see his joy the next day, and he gave me a bible and told me to pray and read it every day.

So that is what I did and God started to speak to me. I know that sounds strange, but I asked God about things in my life and He answered clearly. Marijuana was one of the first things, "Why is it wrong to smoke it?" and was directed to Isaiah chapter 55. *'Come, all you who are thirsty, come to the waters; and you who have no money, come, buy and eat! Come, buy wine and milk without money and without cost. Why spend money on that which is not bread, and your labour on that which does not satisfy? Listen, listen to me, and eat what is good, and you will delight in the richest of fare.'* It blew my mind and I stopped smoking weed instantly. I then prayed that God would help me stop smoking and felt the Holy Spirit in my chest, a kind of warm feeling, and no longer craved a cigarette. Miraculous stuff was happening, and, in my true 'full on' nature, I wanted more. I started telling my friends and family about Jesus and received a mixed response. I guess some of them thought I'd gone mad, but, on the whole, people respectfully listened. Cez suggested that we should find a church to attend so we went to his parents' place of worship, Calvary Baptist. This was such a new experience for me and I was filled with nervous anticipation. Up to now, I had naively viewed the church as a place full of losers. Punk rock had many songs ripping religion apart, and I had largely believed the hype. I don't remember that first service I sat through, but I felt God's presence there and afterwards, a lady came over to talk to me. I felt like a baby in as much as I didn't know what to say to her. I spoke to a few people there and could see their joy at what had happened to me.

After a few weeks, Cez remembered a church in Riverside he had attended years before, and we ventured there one Sunday. On walking through their doors, my heart exploded. There were about 30 people, mostly of Caribbean descent, all clapping, jumping around with tambourines and praising God. It was a party, and I immediately felt that I was in a place I wanted to be in. After the service, we were overpowered by most of the congregation. They wanted to know who we were and hear our stories. The pastor approached us wearing the biggest smile and introduced himself as Pastor Marshall. He was a man full of joy; you could almost see the love he had for people pouring from his heart. There were quite a few people our age there, and I probably knew straight away that I was going to make this place my spiritual home.

A life I never knew existed began to unfold before me. We immersed ourselves in our new-found faith. Our songwriting had changed and we held an all-night prayer meeting at our house, stuff I would have never have dreamt of myself doing. I learnt that we were brothers and sisters in God's family and scripture compelled me to act and talk in a brand-new way. My social life changed, Monday was choir practice, Tuesday bible study and we met in each other's houses regularly in between. We were baptised within a matter of weeks. I recall many of our friends came and Monk, who is a staunch atheist, was holding my towel as I came out of the water. I'll never forget the big smile on his face as he said to me, "I don't believe in any of this but I'm so happy for you." As an immature Christian, I was making many mistakes when I spoke to people about my faith. I felt I lacked something until one evening at choir practice. On Monday's we would meet in the church as 'young people' to pray and make music together. That night, myself and Cez were sitting watching Melvyn playing the guitar and singing when we experienced an almighty warmth and a powerful sensation flowing through us. We looked at each other saying, "Did you feel that?" We found out that we had been baptised in the Spirit. From that day on I could feel God's power and authority in me when I spoke.

Then, after a while, Cez announced he was leaving for London. I was disappointed in a selfish way as this wasn't the first time I had lost a close friend to a foreign destination, however, he was going to college and my life was so full I took it well. He left and, for some reason shortly after, I stopped going to church. I can't even remember what I was doing instead as I had largely stopped all the activities of old.

After two weeks of not going to Shiloh there was a knock on my door. I was living on my own then so it was easy to avoid people. I answered and found myself face to face with Vaz, a brother from Shiloh. "Where have you been?" he asked. I have forgotten my excuse. "Jump in my car and let's go to my house," so I did. Vaz wasn't the type to argue with, he carried a certain authority but also, I had a sense that we had plenty in common. I left for his house around 9.00 pm and got home at 4.00am. He only lived a mile or so up the road and once there, we talked and talked and then did some more talking. We bonded quickly, sharing stories of our old lives and realising that we had the same sense of humour. After that night, I returned to church and would spend many nights at Vaz's, reading the scriptures and talking about anything and everything. He had quickly become the 'new Cez' in my life.

I was beginning to have dreams like never before. I saw a friend of ours, Tim, who had been shot dead in Italy, standing before me with his chest blown open. I began to become aware of a 'visitor' to my room when I was asleep. I could see myself lying in bed as a shadow stood behind me but felt no threat from it. Then, one night, I had a vivid vision of a demon coming at me, a hairy one with a broken arm, and I remember being afraid. I gathered myself in the dream and rebuked it in the name of Jesus, and it retreated. It came back a few times after that, but I was learning to fight it. Then I was at a party talking to a girl I didn't know about Christ when she looked me in the eye, with a menacing stare and said, "Yeah, I'm a born-again Christian." I awoke immediately, only to feel the most powerful force of evil in my room. I was trembling and fell out of bed onto my hands and knees, praying. It subsided. I had watched many horror films in my life before and was familiar with that feeling of being scared, but this was something tenfold to that. Once when I was visiting Cez in London, I went to an African church where there was a Prophet calling people out as he prophesied. He said that there was someone in the building who had been having a visitor, and if they came forward, he would tell them who it was. I knew he was speaking to me, but I froze in my seat, reluctant to go to the front before about 500 people. I never found out about the shadow.

At work, travelling from shop to shop, I was telling everyone I worked with about Jesus and my new-found life. I had been renamed Reverend Denton by my colleagues. Below my house was a shop that I'd work in now and again, managed by a lady called Dawn. I would often go down and sit with her in the mornings when it was quiet and have a coffee with her. She appeared to love the company even though I spent most of the time talking about the bible. She had many different cashiers work with her, but one day, a young girl from Swansea, Tina, was there. She showed a particular interest in what I was saying. She was an art student and, in my eyes, very talented. She had painted an impressive mural in the shop. Cez had returned from London for a visit over the summer, and we had planned a concert in the church. We needed a poster, so I asked her if she would design it for us, to which she agreed. I spent more time with her outside of the shop as she only lived over the road. She held a genuine interest in what I was saying and eventually I bought her a bible. She told me she cried when I did this.

Due to the size of the church, my accumulated life skills were soon utilised. Pastor Marshall was a man who believed in involving people and allowing them to express themselves. I started playing bass during the praise and worship. A talented keyboardist led this, Debbie, and she would call out the notes for me as we went along, as I was unfamiliar with the songs. I ditched my plectrum and started to learn to play with my fingers. I was called on to pray in front of the church and thought nothing of it, and, eventually, was asked to preach. This was a milestone. I had been studying and living out the scriptures for quite a while by then, but was extremely nervous. I prepared a message at home from Genesis about sin. I remember waiting for the call from the pastor to speak, wracked with nerves. I had made some notes to help guide me. Sermons often lasted between half an hour and an hour and I thought I had enough material to speak for roughly that long. However, I stood up in the pulpit, rattled out the message from my notes and finished. Pastor Marshall glanced up when I announced this and, in his typically joyful style, said 'Very good, Stef. I had spoken for approximately five minutes! My spiritual family were very kind after, saying that the message had enough substance in it and that it didn't matter how long I spoke for. They were probably right, but I felt a shade embarrassed. I spoke many times after this and started taking bible studies as my knowledge of the Word grew. My confidence also grew with the experiences, and eventually, I was able to speak for much longer. So, as was my way, things were moving at an explosive pace into a new life, and more blessings were just around the corner.

After a short while of friendship, I asked Tina out on a date. I'd had a couple of flings since Justine, but this was the first time that I'd actually dated a girl. We went to a local curry house, and Tina recounts that she was so nervous she had drunk a bottle of wine before she called over. It didn't really show, but as I was gulping my food down, I noticed she was barely eating. Our relationship grew, and so I invited her to church, and she accepted.

Tina was welcomed and loved by my church family and soon found her place. During one Sunday Service, Tina vanished into the toilets with Jackie, the Pastor's daughter. Afterwards, having wondered what had happened, she told me she had given her life to Jesus Christ and was now a Christian. I was overjoyed, and we talked about our love for each other and the possibility of marriage. I'd always been pretty awful and awkward in relationships, and rather than propose in the traditional manner, it was more of a 'discussion'. We agreed that it was what we wanted and so set a date for that summer. We set about planning it on a small, if hardly existent, budget, but drew plenty of help from the members of our church. Sister Padmore made the cake and some of the other older ladies chipped in. My naivety started to shine through and I booked a room at Channel View Leisure Centre for our reception, which wasn't the best move. The most we spent was probably on our honeymoon, where, having discussed it with Andy, we decided to go and stay with him in California. By now, she was discovering her talents in church, as I had, and one Monday evening at choir practice, her voice came to the fore.

The Shiloh Singers, as we were known, had started singing in various places. We were invited to weddings, other churches, youth clubs, the Mal Pope show on Radio Wales and Songs of Praise on the BBC. We became quite well-known in the Cardiff area and it was clear to see that God was opening doors for us to minister. We married in August 1995 and Tina moved in with me in Penylan Road and we began our new life together.

FROM THE RISING OF THE SUN...

Meanwhile, during all this, I began to feel that my time was up at the bookies. During youth meetings on Wednesday, it often came up that I shouldn't be working in a 'den of iniquity' as it was put. One brother in particular had a problem with it, as if it were him living it out, but I knew God wanted me there up to this point. I prayed about it and, shortly after, saw that the YMCA were looking for volunteers. I went over to their building in The Walk and sat with a lady called Jan, who talked to me and said I would be a welcome addition to their team.

Foolishly, I paid no thought to money and handed my notice in at William Hill and began work at the YMCA on a pittance, which left us short at home. I had freedom there to develop my own projects and, in the course of time, began playing football in the small gym they had with some of the residents. This became really popular and, in an effort to make it more interesting, I phoned other similar organisations asking if they could put together 5-a-side teams to meet and play at Channel View. Within a few short weeks, teams from The Wallich Clifford, Tresillian House, The Huggard Centre and The YMCA were meeting there and having mini competitions.

I was learning several new skills in the YMCA and became aware that computers were becoming a big part of the world. There was a computer room opposite my office, so I would find an empty computer every day and teach myself Microsoft Word, Excel and Publisher. As a project to help me learn, I wrote anonymous letters to Monk telling him that 'we were aware of his habits' and that he was 'being monitored'. After sending a few of these out, I paid him a brief visit. In the course of our catching up, he told me about them and brought them down from upstairs, where he kept them completely clueless about their origin. This pleased me as I would have been one of the first suspects on Monk's list years before, but I guess he didn't realise I had learned to type. I did eventually reveal it to him, but I can't remember what he said. Knowing Monk, he probably swore at me!

Such was its popularity as an amateur sport, I began wondering why there were no 5-a-side football leagues or competitions in Cardiff. So I called the South Wales Echo and told them I was starting a 5-a-side league. They ran a small article the next day, but I was unprepared for the response. The YMCA's switchboard lit up! Within a week, I had over forty phone calls from interested parties. One call was from the Football Association of Wales, who rang me to find out who I was and what I intended to do. I told them I was working for a charity and that all money raised would go to them. Clueless but knowing I was on to something big, I arranged for five teams to meet every Thursday evening at Channel View and play each other in a round robin. This went on for about a year and I learned a great deal, although I had not given any thought to finely tuning the idea. I also suffered doubts at times, thinking to myself, 'who was I to be doing such a thing?' and other thoughts crept in, attacking my confidence and whether it was 'God's will'. I had very little support from staff, as I don't think they realised the enormity of what was happening. The accounts manager did ask me once about it, as, originally, he had been recording it as 'petty cash', but said he didn't expect so much income and needed to re-categorise it.

Then, one night whilst reading the Echo, I spotted a small advert by a company called Leisure Leagues who were looking to hire a '5-a-side league manager'. I called them to find out who they were and the man I spoke to, Pete, said they were based near Coventry and would be visiting Cardiff. He arranged to meet up with me and discuss what they did as a company.

At the time, I was producing a weekly pamphlet, using my new-found skills on Microsoft Publisher, of fixtures, tables and results of games played (going back to my Subbuteo days) and took a copy along to the meeting. Pete and another gentleman, David, met me and seemed impressed by my setup, but said that they ran their leagues in a different way so if I came to work for them, I would have to adapt to their methods. That was fine by me and having looked at what they did, it made more sense. A date was set for me to start, and I returned to the YMCA to tell them.

By this time, I had been there a few years and had acquired a position in the Chief Executive's office doing administration. My former boss, Roy, came into the office, and I told him and John, the Chief Executive, that I would be working for Leisure Leagues and the YMCA would be losing my project. John hit the roof. He had been completely unaware of how successful the 5-a-side had become and saw it as an opportunity missed. It was a bit late then, though, and I began to discuss the idea with the teams who were playing regularly under my old format. I formed a new league at the Welsh Institute of Sport comprising a few new teams. Under Leisure Leagues' new rules and structure, it improved and soon word was getting around. I began branching out, starting some new leagues in Neath and Cwmbran and expanded the income, working towards full-time employment. This eventually came and so I handed in my notice at the YMCA. I produced a weekly programme with all the leagues in. It included the fixtures, results and tables and on the back page, I would write a message of God's grace and goodness, which I would change every week. This was distributed so that each team had a copy.

A few years previously, a couple of American ladies had visited our church, for which we held a special meeting. They were prophesying over people at this service and when they called me out, I was told that I would "take the word to the South and the East." At the time, I didn't understand this and wondered sometimes if it meant I was going to be a preacher, but one day, while standing at my kitchen sink washing dishes, God revealed to me that the programme was the fulfilment of the prophecy. That blew my mind!

In July 1996, my first son was born, and we named him Luke. Tina had come to see me in the YMCA nine months previous, and when she broke the news, I was ecstatic. I couldn't believe what the Lord was doing in my life, a wife and now a child. I was 31 and had never seen myself as the type to have a family and 'settle down'. However, I had become a 'new creation' and, in February 1996, had moved to a small house in Fairwater, ready for our new arrival. I learned to drive for my job, another thing I had given no thought to, and started working from home. I also received my first mobile phone. They were few and far between at the time, and I found it quite embarrassing when it rang with people around, apologising for the interruption. Almost two years later, my second son arrived on the scene and we named him Malachi. Our life together was blessed, and with work thriving and more and more leagues starting, the future looked bright.

In the year 2000, I employed a man whom I had known in high school, Steve. The number of leagues had grown to about 12 by now, so I had been given authorisation to take him on to run the leagues in order to concentrate on further business developments. A building in Swansea that had previously been a football centre was now vacant, and I caught wind of it through my league manager in the area. I suggested to my bosses at HQ that we should take a look at leasing the building and expanding our operation. They came down and, after talking it through, decided they would look into it. It didn't take long before work had begun to turn it into Leisure Leagues' first indoor football centre. It opened later that year, and I travelled down daily to manage it, occasionally staying all week at my mother-in-law's, who lived in Swansea. So I went from spending the first few years of my kids' lives working at home and being with them to spending pretty much all week in Swansea, meaning I saw less and less of them and Tina. This put great strain on her and eventually, one Sunday, I woke up exhausted and suggested that we give church a miss. She agreed. Neither of us knew that the decision we made that day was the start of a downward slippery slope.

I was completely consumed by work, and we started going to church less and less. After a year of the Swansea centre running successfully, I persuaded Leisure Leagues to look at having a similar setup in Cardiff and in 2001, they took out a lease on a building in Curran Road. This was my dream by then, to return to Cardiff to work.

...TO THE GOING DOWN OF THE SAME

By 2002, Steve and I were working flat out to build the business in the new arena, keeping an eye on the Swansea arena where I had employed a new manager and running the 25 leagues we had around Wales and parts of England. God had truly blessed the work of my hands, but I was going to church less and less and was so distracted that I possibly didn't see the cracks that were appearing in my life. I was hardly praying or spending time in God's word by now. The programme I had produced for my leagues no longer carried a weekly message, and I had come up with no way of integrating it into the arenas. This had troubled me at first, but after a while, I forgot about it. I remember having a visit at the arena from one of the brothers from the church, but told him I was too busy to fellowship. At home, Tina seemed unconcerned and rarely, if ever, spoke about church. She had met some new friends through the kids' nursery and seemed keen to hide her past life from them. She was beginning to develop a new social life with them, one she had never really had in her youth.

I don't remember why, but one day I went and knocked on Monk's door. This was sometime in late 2003. I had hardly seen him for the last eight years or more, but I wondered what he was doing with his life. After reminiscing for a while, he showed me the marijuana people were smoking now that had become common since my smoking days...bud. Back in the day, we smoked 'solids', a variety of different resins squeezed into a block. Proper bud or 'green' as it was called was only a pipe dream. I had smoked some in California when visiting Andy, but it was generally not available to the British public. In my weakness and state of spiritual decline, temptation overcame my self-control. I suggested that I try one, convincing both Monk and myself that, because it had been so long since I last had involvement, I could easily stop at that. In fairness, Monk did his utmost to convince me it wasn't the best idea, but that did little to discourage me. I smoked that day and was taken back in time with a bit extra thrown in. I left his place after the effects had worn off and returned home, telling Tina what I had done. She put up little resistance to it, probably not realising what was about to unfold. I returned to see Monk the next night and the next, and after a few days of this, so as not to become a pest, asked him to get me some. I was well and truly hooked again.

From that experience, I went to a card night that the old crew were still having, but with some new faces. I was quickly developing my old habits and also started venturing back into the world of horse racing, thinking how much fun it would be to have a bet after all this time. God did not leave me alone and often I battled my conscience, learning to push God aside in my mind and, hardening my heart, I justified my actions to myself, thinking that, at any time I pleased, I could take control of my situation and return to my faith. This was a lie, and I could feel the devil laughing in triumph in the background. At work, Steve, who was a bit of a womaniser, was bringing a steady flow of girls he was dating to meet me. He would often cheat on them and, having become his close friend as well as colleague, I would know what he was up to. I didn't interfere, though, probably because I felt little attachment to those girls but would often warn him that his ways would only bring him trouble.

One day, around 2004, he brought in a girl called Angie, blonde, flicked hair and a big smile. On meeting her, I immediately took to her bubbly personality and happy disposition. He was with her a few months, which was quite a while for him, when he told me that he had 'messed about' with another girl. Unlike before, I was mad at him, threatening to inflict violence on him if he hurt her. I had become acquainted with Angie as we had all gone out with friends for meals, and she had come along with Steve. I had grown fond of her as a friend and knew a small piece of her background, which wasn't all good. After a while, they split up, not in the best fashion, and I called at her house to see how she was. We sat over coffee, getting to know each other and sharing stories of our lives. I would tell her of my faith and try to explain that, as much as I believed, I wasn't living it out at the moment. I met her two young daughters, Emma and Hannah, and found that Emma especially liked to discuss God with me. Then, one evening, I went around Angie's on a social visit and we talked over some weed and wine. She, I learned quickly, loved wine. When the time came to leave, we had a comforting cuddle on her sofa, and I departed. I had no intention of cheating on Tina, faithfulness was one of the few things remaining in our marriage, and I didn't need any more complications in my life then. The next day, I had a text from Angie saying something like she was glad I hadn't stayed any longer, as we might have ended up in bed together.

Slowly and subtly, Tina and I had developed new, separate social lives, although sometimes we would mingle together, but we were becoming nothing more than babysitters for each other. Tina largely lived upstairs, and I lived down. We didn't argue or complain but quietly went about our business with little or no concern as to what the other was doing. My week became steadfast, Pedro's on Monday for smoking and backgammon, cards on Tuesday for smoking with the boys and out smoking somewhere on Friday. Tina also had her fixed nights, but Saturday was when she went out with the girls and came home worse for wear. Our kids seemed happy, as life must have been normal to them. They had both parents living together, regular visits to both grandparents, and we would take them out separately to do things. One of our passions was to play golf. I took them to Heath Park to play at least once a week, and they were both involved in junior football sides. Among all this, me and Tina were becoming strangers and, as we headed toward the end of the decade of being married, she began asking me to leave. I struggled with this at first. I couldn't bear the thought of leaving my kids and when she told me to "find somewhere else to live", I would reply, "no, you find somewhere else to live."

I was, at this point in my life, earning more money than I ever had but due to my extravagant lifestyle, found myself sinking further and further into debt. Credit cards and bank loans meant nothing to me and the interest, as anyone who has been there knows, made things worse. My job was turning sour as well. I began feeling as if my bosses wanted rid of me, but wasn't sure if that was true or just paranoia. I suddenly wanted out and, in making another rash decision, handed my notice in. My dream job was just thrown away on a whim. For the next year of my life, I was lost. I had no idea what to do for work and having just lost a position of such power was learning to humble myself again. I had been to the job centre but found them no help, eventually cutting them off and losing all the benefits I had been entitled to. My nights were spent getting stoned and days gambling, believing falsely that I was good enough to make a living from it. By 2007, I could see no way out and, after much thought and deliberation, decided to go bankrupt. It made me feel ashamed of myself. I had no mortgage and very few possessions, which made it an easy course of action, and it brought me to the decision that I would never owe money to anyone again. I had reached a low point in my life and, for what turned out to be about three months, went back to my faith. I repented, prayed and went back to church.

It was then that one of the brothers, Eugene, asked if I was interested in becoming a carer as the company he worked for was looking for new staff. How hard could that be? I took on the challenge and went to meet the manager, Cathy. I recall saying to her that I knew how forceful and pushy to the staff care companies were (Tina had been a carer briefly when we were first together) and there was no way I was going to be pushed around. I was given my first rota, which was basically a list of names and addresses, and sent out on a Friday night to work. It was only my life skills and experience that got me through that night. I couldn't believe what they had sent me into with no training or advice and it played hell on Monday. In the few years I worked there, I was loud and argumentative, accusing them of loving money more than the clients and could see the look in their eyes whenever I walked into the office. They must have dreaded it, although, having said that, I had a good rapport with most of them, especially Cathy, who was a good manager. A few years later, I was asked to train a new employee, a man ten years older than myself, another Steve, and within a shift, we had become good friends. My induction involved telling him what working for the company was really like…my version! I found out that he was like-minded and would speak his mind. We bonded quickly and became good friends.

It wasn't very long after that the council announced a big 'shake up' in the care system and were threatening to close many companies. Steve and I found out about a charity called 'Diverse Cymru' where clients (or service users as the system calls them) could cut out the middleman and directly employ carers. We discussed with four of our favourite clients moving to this arrangement and took them to Diverse Cymru, covering all their calls and needs, enlisting the help of a few people we knew. It was a far better way to work and I was really enjoying working alongside Steve. At home, things had come to a head. Tina was demanding more and more that I leave and as the kids had reached the ages of 13 and 11, I decided that I had to oblige. It was a heartbreaking moment in my life when we sat them down to tell them. The question was 'Where would I go?' I had thought about my parents, which seemed like the only option, but I needed my own space.

It was then that I was in conversation with a friend of my youth, Kate. I had met Kate when I was about 18. She was friends with my first girlfriend, Beccy and we shared a love of books. We had, off and on, kept in touch. Kate had travelled for much of her life, living in various towns and cities and had a love of Australia but I would always track her down when we lost touch. Anyway, I was telling Kate about my predicament when she presented a temporary solution. She was about to go to Australia for a few months and needed someone to look after her house in Elm Street. She offered me rent-free accommodation if I fancied taking on the task. I was over the moon! Now, some say life deals us lucky moments or, as Pedro put it, "he's landed on his feet again!" but I believe that God offers provision within his plan for us. I have seen this many times throughout my life.

FEMALE FRIENDS

On the last day of November 2010, I packed my few belongings and moved in with Kate. She wasn't leaving until just before Christmas but had a big house and plenty of room. I will never forget my first night there, lying in bed crying and feeling the dreadful sense of absence I had left in my kids' lives. I have always had a 'quick healing' heart, though and often wondered if it had something to do with my experience as a baby. It wasn't long before I became, in my mind, eighteen again. Kate had given me approximately four months before she had plans to sell the house. Her intention was to move to Australia and she was going to set her plans in motion on her return. During this period, I fell in love with both my newfound freedom and the house I had been gifted. In March 2011, I was speaking to an old friend when she told me of some trouble she had been having with her boyfriend, whom she was living with. I asked her if she wanted to come and live with me after discussing renting the place with Kate. It was affordable, and Kate said that although she would be selling the house, she was willing to rent it to me for a while. She moved in during April.

Within two weeks, I was looking for somewhere else. My new housemate wasn't the tidiest, and I found myself going through an experience I didn't expect. She had suffered at the hands of her previous boyfriend and had become a little damaged. After ditching the idea of moving out, we began talking about her problems and slowly we found a better place together. My bible came out, and I would read her scripture and pray for her situation to improve. Slowly, it did. Then, out of the blue, Cez contacted me and said he had been in touch on Facebook with our old friend Beano, who had recently become a Christian.

Incredible news! I looked him up on Facebook and arranged for him to come down and tell me his story. In the 30 years since I'd last seen him, he had become one of South Wales's most wanted criminals. He told me tales that shocked me, a life of high crime. He was feared by many, and his name was infamous, especially around the Pontypridd area. It made me recall a time in the Model Inn years previous when two guys started getting a bit aggressive with me. I noticed their Welsh accents and asked them where they were from, to which they replied, "Ponty." I proceeded to tell them I knew a guy called Beano from up that way, and their whole attitudes changed. Turns out that one day, Beano had been challenged by someone he knew to go on an Alpha Course. This is a basic Christian course that explores the faith and allows people to ask questions. Beano had gone with the intention to prove the whole thing as rubbish and cause disruption, but, on week eight, surrendered his life to Jesus Christ.

My housemate had warmed to the gospel, expressing a desire to go to church, a place I hadn't been for a long time. My love for God had begun to return and the time I was spending with the Word and in prayer began to rejuvenate me. She went to visit her brother for three weeks in November and, whilst away, I once again stopped reading and praying. By the time she came back, I was finding her ways annoying again, perhaps born from the simplicity of living on my own, having my own space. Our relationship fell apart and within a month, I told her that she had to leave. Kate was of the opinion that she would sell the house, so it all seemed to make sense. In January 2012, my parents had gone to America themselves, so I moved into their house to keep an eye on it and left her to clear up her belongings to move out. We were barely talking, which saddened me. I rang Cez in London to get a Christian perspective on the whole thing. My heart was deeply troubled as I'd never argued or lost an old friend in this way before, and questioned my own behaviour. I went to see Cam for comfort and more justification that I hadn't acted unreasonably. In that meeting, she told me that she had had enough of living in the area she was in and had been giving some thought to moving herself. This naturally led to us discussing her moving into Elm Street with me if I could convince Kate to allow us. I considered how it would look when my old friend found out, as if I had lied about the reason for kicking her out, but then, with nowhere else to go myself, realised that tough decisions have to be made sometimes.

Besides, she had somewhere else safe to go.

Kate agreed to extend our stay for a while, and Cam moved in around March 2012. She was a breath of fresh air, quickly turning the house into a home. She filled the place with pictures on the wall and plants in the garden, things I never gave a thought to. I started to have my kids over to stay on weekends and life began to pick up once more. I still went to Pedro's on Monday for a backgammon session and, in a conversation with him about my work, told him I was beginning to struggle with the late finishes and working weekends. He had recently started his own company and was toying with the idea of taking on an administrator or office manager. It was a nine-to-five, Monday to Friday, full-time job, hours I hadn't worked for a long time. It would free me up for a different social life and weekends with the kids, so I sat down with Steve and asked if he could find someone to take over from me. Thankfully, he was fine and understood my reasons for leaving. One client, however, he didn't want to take on was Lyz. I had taken Lyz on whilst working for my previous company. I walked into the office one day and found a few of the girls arguing with the manager. None of the staff wanted to take on Lyz's call, and Cathy looked at me and said, "Here's the man for the job." I agreed to do it and hit it off with Lyz immediately. I understood why the girls didn't want the call, but it was a matter of learning how Lyz liked things and how to manage her. I had to find someone to take Lyz off my hands as I would no longer be able to do her call if I was to accept the job from Pedro. I thought of Angie, who, apart from her full-time job, had some hours as a carer, so went to discuss it with her over coffee, and she agreed. Lyz also seemed happy with this arrangement.

By now, my kids had the same passion for horse racing as myself so I planned out a week away with them, touring some of Britain's racecourses. My early ambition of visiting them all was about to take a steep upward climb. That summer we set off in the car and went to Uttoxeter, York, Carlisle, Ayr and finished in Perth. It was an amazing experience where we saw a fair amount of England and Scotland's beautiful landscapes. I hadn't given any thought to the mileage and returned home a week later, exhausted from a 1,500-mile adventure. The kids loved it, and it was the first time in years I had gone away with them.

This was to become an annual trip. In the back of my mind, as always, my conscience pricked me. I was encouraging and fuelling gambling in my kids' lives, which was not good and knew that, if not kept under control, could end up cursing them.

In truth, so much about my life really bothered me. When you find God, no matter where you go or what you do, He is there loving you, speaking to you and gently reminding you that His ways are better. We are accountable for our actions to Him. The choices we make affect and influence others and compel them to make right or wrong decisions. My kids were my responsibility and a gift from Him, and here I was teaching them all the wrong things. I would still talk to God and tell Him how worried and disgusted I was to be living like this. My heart was becoming harder and harder for Him as the years went by. Even on the ever-so-brief occasions I tried to wrestle my faith back, I fell again soon after. I prayed and called out, saying, "What can I do about this? What can ever happen to bring me back to you?"

YOU NEVER KNOW
WHAT'S AROUND THE CORNER

Here I was heading full on to being 50 years of age, in a house I loved, albeit with an edge of insecurity, living with a friend I loved. Cam came home one day and told me she had bumped into an old friend of ours, Grayam, whom I hadn't seen for about 25 years. Grayam was a punk back in the day, and we knew each other loosely through our social circles, sharing the same sense of humour as I remember. She had invited him to call around and share memories of old times and so he did. It turned out that Grayam had recently been learning to play guitar and had written numerous riffs with a head full of lyrics he didn't know what to do with. I hadn't played bass for years and didn't even own one, but, on hearing his songs, fell in love with them and wanted to be involved. I went out and bought a basic bass and amp over Splott market and invited him to call around to see what we could put together. We gelled and began to construct songs in the most natural way. He had great talent in my eyes and a fantastic voice. His songs were simple but powerful, but he lacked ideas on how to structure them. This was my gift and so we began to quickly amass a catalogue of tunes, practising regularly in each other's houses and spending many nights together getting stoned and jamming. We would talk at length about our lives and share intimate secrets, bonding in both friendship and music. We played a couple of gigs together in Pontypridd, meeting up with old friends Beva and Sian, who had their own band, Vinna Bee. A romantic summer of music and friendship was being ignited and I was loving my life with only the occasional thought of God and His plan for me.

In the early months of 2013, we hooked up with Tom and Ally, whom I'd never met before but were friends of Grayam. They had their own band and a studio in their house. Tom was a drummer and Ally sang, so we started developing our sound with them. Tom, when we started, explained that their band was the priority for them. I understood in part, but as an excitable type was thrilled to be making music again and threw myself headfirst into the project. Our songs were, in my mind, some of the best I had ever been involved in writing. Grayam and I were doing everything together and would spend at least four nights a week talking and jamming with band practice on a Sunday. Once ready, after a couple of months of practice, we booked the Royal Oak on Broadway for a gig to raise money for the foodbank. On the bill were us, Inastruggle, Beva and Sian's band, Vinna Bee and Tom and Ally's D-Teez. The place was packed that night and there were people who couldn't get into the room we were playing in. It was a great success, and we talked proudly about the tremendous feedback we received from everyone there. Shortly after, I went back to the Royal Oak to book another, which would incorporate Cez's band, who agreed to come down from London. When discussing this with the manager, he asked if the first band that played would come back as he really liked them. "That's my band," I proudly announced. I turned up at practice and announced this to the others, and got the feeling they were unimpressed by something.

I left to go on tour with my boys that week. We travelled to Brighton, Lingfield, Newmarket, Norwich, Great Yarmouth and Huntingdon before returning home. An easier and more compact trip than the previous year, and was in communication with Grayam while away. I was still buzzing and on a high from that gig, and my ego had been fed by the whole experience. I soon learned that Tom and Ally were not best pleased by the way I had gone about things. I felt ashamed by my behaviour and went over to their place to apologise. For some reason, they wouldn't let me in, and I left with an overpowering sense of disappointment. I mean, we all make mistakes, don't we? Grayam told me that it was over and my heart hit the floor. I had lost a lover, or at least that's how it felt, and I struggled to deal with it, walking around in misery. I don't think I had ever been so consumed with sadness and despair before in my life and I spent the next two months being miserable before I got over it.

In the midst of all this, I had been visiting Angie, who had now moved nearby. She was having a bad time in her relationship, which was now in its tenth year and we arranged to take Lyz out for a curry together. We had a good night, and I enjoyed spending time with her and Lyz, so we agreed to do it again. The second time I dropped Angie home, I went in for a coffee. She had become more aggrieved with her situation and we sat talking on the sofa with her partner sleeping upstairs. She began to pour her heart out to me and I would do my best to encourage her. Then, in a moment of madness, she grabbed my head and kissed me. At first, I was shocked, but I couldn't deny enjoying it. But she had a boyfriend, and there was no way I wanted this complication. The next day, she texted me apologising, but I told her not to worry. We arranged to go out for a curry again with Lyz. In my shame, I loved Lyz, but she became a kind of excuse for us to meet up socially, although she appreciated the company.

We went back to my house after dropping Lyz home, and there I confessed to really liking her but was wary that she was in a relationship and didn't want to break that up. She knew that was over and told me that he was moving out. We kissed again and, in a moment of high passion, almost took things further. Angie managed to gather herself, and I dropped her home.

Once she had dealt with her recently dissolved relationship, I started to call over and spend the evening with her a couple of times a week. I remember saying, "I enjoy your company," repeating it until she told me to shut up. We shared our stories of who we were and how we had grown up and I soon realised that she carried plenty of pain and grief from her rough upbringing. Her father had abused her in many ways and left her

psychologically damaged. I wanted to help her and tried my best to talk about it, but found that large parts of her were protected by the walls she had built up in her heart. I began to fall for her; she had the bravest outlook considering what she had been through. I admired the life she had made for herself from her terrible start she'd had, her unconditional love of her two girls, Emma and Hannah, whom I had known loosely for quite some time now and in a teenage kind of way, asked her if she would be my girlfriend. It was the beginning of October 2013. She said 'yes'. We were very different people and would clash over many things. She had experience of a Catholic Church which often clashed with my biblical beliefs but something drew us to each other and, at this point, neither of us could figure out what.

Her daughter, Hannah, who lived with her, commented on why her mother was with me. She could probably see that her mother was with a man who was a bit different, strange as she put it. Their household was not what I was used to, inasmuch as Hannah and Angie would explode into arguments over nothing, shouting and screaming at each other. It took some getting used to on my behalf as I would have to sit in silence. It was none of my business and I didn't want to be dragged in. Things moved slowly at first. I was sitting on my own in Elm Street one Saturday night watching telly, stoned, when Angie texted me asking what I was doing. "Nothing really", I sent back and she thought it strange that we were in separate houses alone when we could have been together. I still loved my private life and didn't want to jump into a full-blown relationship. I struggled at times with our differences and questioned myself whether we should be together and remember thinking, because we were so different, we were doomed. At the same time, I carried guilt and was wary because the last thing I wanted to do was hurt her.

Her group of best friends were called 'The Motley Crew' and she told me that each year around November, they booked a hotel in Torquay and spent the weekend together. Angie asked me if I wanted to go with her. I didn't really know what to say. I discussed it with Cam as it was something I hadn't done before in my life and had mixed feelings. As you know by now, music and marijuana formed a large part of my daily life, and we had very different tastes in music, and Angie would never touch the 'wacky backy', her poison was alcohol. I had a big dislike of pubs and environments involving alcohol as I found them loud and lairy. It was an event that could end disastrously as she, and I was guessing, her friends were so different to me and would spend the weekends drinking. I dwelt on it for a while and decided to go, nervously hoping that it wouldn't end in tears.

HALF A CENTURY ON PLANET EARTH

That trip to Torquay cemented our relationship. Her friends were very welcoming and easy to get on with. On the first night, we had our room broken into. Our finances had been stripped from us, leaving us with nothing but her friends soon rallied to the cause. They had a 'whip around' to help us get through the weekend, and my heart warmed to their acts of kindness. It was the first time we had spent days together and our relationship began to flourish as we found ourselves in the honeymoon period. We were still mystified by our attraction to one another, but I was developing a feeling of love to match the admiration I already had for this girl. She gave me a sense of purpose, and I wallowed in her apparent love and need to have me around. Angie was a well-guarded person when it came to emotions, but was an expert at making you feel wanted and at ease around her. We returned home, and I told Cam of my unusual experience. She told me to 'go with it'.

Our first Christmas together came soon after. I was spending Christmas Day with my parents, but went down to Angie's that evening to exchange small presents we had bought one another and six days later, we spent my birthday and New Year's Eve watching Jools Holland, a tradition we would keep from that year on. In 2014, and I was spending more evenings at her house, although I never stayed, I felt that it wasn't right with her daughter living there. Friday nights, she would stay at Elm Street. I cooked a curry for us whilst she enjoyed her bottle of wine and I smoked my stuff. We watched rubbish on TV together and talked for hours in bed, often sharing a tub of ice cream. Sometime that year, I told her "I loved her", to which she would become embarrassed. We hadn't thought of or discussed the matter but Angie would make it clear that she had sworn never to marry anyone ever again and I believed her. All too often, though, in the midst of an innocent evening together, we would have a difference of opinion and storm out of each other's houses, somehow managing to make up shortly after. It was a rocky relationship to say the least, but we couldn't let each other go. Another surprising thing happened in early 2014. Cez called me, telling me he was coming back to live in Cardiff. I was over the moon! He had been gone for over twenty years and the thought of having him around filled me with both happiness and a sense of dread. God was lingering around my thoughts as always and I would feel a conviction when in the presence of other Christians because of my sinful lifestyle. I had avoided Vaz for years.

In 2015, Cez and Michelle, who had been back in Cardiff a while, moved into their new house and I took Angie around to meet them. She had met Cez once before when he had visited me a few years earlier but our relationship was in its infancy then. By the time we left, Angie and Michelle had become good friends. Michelle is careful about who she lets into her life but they seemed to easily strike up a friendship. From that day, we would meet up regularly for meals and social talk but any mention of faith in God was at a minimum. Cez had a set of songs from his previous band and suggested that we renew our past glories of songwriting. We started jamming in his house and quickly put together some lovely tunes.

He sent them to an old friend who was a drummer and he expressed an interest in working with us. Cam was drafted in as, initially, a backing singer and we booked a rehearsal room. Within the space of five or six months, we had a well-tuned set and recorded a demo. We were ready to go and present ourselves to the world. We took the recordings home with us and soon began receiving discontent messages from Evo, our drummer. It seemed like he wasn't happy with several things and at our next practice, spilled the beans. He loved the music we were creating but on taking the demo home and listening to the lyrics, he became aware that the songs had a Christian theme. As an atheist, he was troubled by this and said he didn't want to be a hypocrite. We understood and, after a lengthy discussion outside the practice room, called it a day. This was the second time in the space of a few years that this had happened to me, except this time I didn't feel that misery. I took it gracefully and moved on. Cez and I packed it in as well. We had other things going on and, if nothing else, had a demo from our experience.

On New Year's Eve 2014, we celebrated my 50th birthday in Elm Street with a couple of friends watching Jools Holland and getting smashed. Our love had grown for each other, but we still had disagreements. Angie worked hard, holding down her full-time job in Kitchener Primary School and working for Barnardos several nights and on Saturdays. It cheesed me off as I wanted her to slow down a bit and have more time for friends and family, so I began paying her to pack in one of her shifts. I was now spending a few nights at her house, as Hannah didn't mind and felt the need to contribute a little. She battled with her wine, often bringing home a bottle from work, saying, "She'd had a bad day." I was smoking every night anyway, so didn't care but knew that she had a habit of trying to start an argument after drinking a bottle. Now and again, she would storm off to bed having picked on me or Hannah and got herself in a tizzy. We loved to book weekends away via Groupon and did occasionally when finances allowed. In the summer of 2015, we went to stay for five days in a cottage in Newport, West Wales. A couple I had worked for owned it and gave us the keys to enjoy a few days away together. We loved that part of the world and always took a trip to St. David's. Fond memories. I'd never done much of this before and was loving our relationship and having someone to share my life with. Angie had a way of convincing me to do things I wouldn't normally do. I'm a stubborn sod at times and can never be told what to do, but she just knew how to make it sound like a good idea, and after doing it, I had to agree.

We were building a meaningful life together. We loved and had good relationships with each other's kids and became accustomed to going out with each other's friends, even though we were quite different. Cez and Michelle's was probably my favourite port of call together, and I was thankful that I could see Cez and that our wives were good friends. Another dynamic in our relationship was that my education and Angie's were worlds apart. I had always admired the fact that she had put herself through school later in life, as she had been denied it as a kid. Her English wasn't good at times, and she had a way of saying things that you couldn't make up. She would often use the word 'thing' to fill in her vocabulary, which would make me laugh, but I would challenge her, hoping to help her improve. In one text, she wrote to her friend regarding a night out, saying, "Looking forward to being severed by the waiter!" She meant 'served', of course. This was not always taken well and she would become arsy with me and tell me to shut up. She often had a problem when I wanted to try and teach her something, but then, at a later date, I would hear her telling the exact same thing to someone else. It gave me comfort and made me laugh.

Looking back through her Facebook posts of that year, and others, I can see that her family and friends, my company and a glass of wine with everything is what she loved. That was one of the things that I loved, her simple ways. She never demanded much from me, she just told me, "You make me laugh every day."

Work-wise, I had finished with Pedro in 2014, done six months of care again and then found a cushy part-time post as a care home administrator. I began cooking every day and changed my diet. I cut out the rubbish that I had been eating for years, and would cook fresh food for me and my parents. I was now living at their house as Kate had sold her house in Elm Street in May 2015, forcing me and Cam to go our separate ways. I had made the decision to move back in with them for a while, as I couldn't really afford my own place and didn't want to move into Angie's. We still weren't quite ready for that. However, I would spend at least five nights a week with her except when I'd gone out to visit friends or to a card night and would come home late. In November, we went for a second year to Torquay, but this time it was not the same. While I enjoyed my time with her, I found it a bit boring sitting watching everyone getting drunk in the evening and by Sunday morning was ready to go home. Angie said we would be staying for dinner and it became more than I could bear. I blew my top in reception, shouting and swearing briefly. Rant over, we loaded the car and set off for Cardiff. The two-hour trip home was painful with neither of us saying a word to each other, me with my shame, and her cheesed off and embarrassed by my behaviour. We were still learning about each other, though and, after an apology on my behalf, quickly resumed our relationship heading into another Christmas.

Angie turned 50 in January 2016 and as I flick through her memories, I see a happy face going to London with her daughters, meeting up with

The Motley Crew and other friends for drinks. This was becoming remarkable territory for me. Tina apart, I had never been with a woman this long and it lays testament to how much we meant to each other at this time, having worked through plenty of disagreements. She had told me once that she never thought, growing up, that anyone would love her. In a post of her 50th celebrations, she wrote, "I feel so loved."

Through that year, she had some wonderful times. She celebrated everyone's birthday as usual with glasses of wine and a big smile, and went on holiday with The Motley Crew in the summer to Turkey. It warmed my heart to know that I was a part of putting that smile on her face. I missed her badly that week and will never forget waiting for her return at the airport. She came running out and jumped on me, giving me a big hug. I felt so loved by her, even if she would rarely tell me. That Christmas, she asked me to spend it at her house with the family. It was her favourite time of year and is summed up by photos of everyone together and a glass of Baileys.

IT MUST BE LOVE

In February 2017, we booked our first holiday abroad together to Iceland. We only had a couple of days there during half term but made the most of this beautiful place. On the second day, we went on a guided tour of the island and our guide, Hauke, was a very interesting and knowledgeable man. I struck it off with him immediately, pouring plenty of questions his way concerning Icelandic history and culture. In the few hours we were with him, I largely left Angie to her own devices. I was torn between the chance to learn and pleasing her, and probably ignored her a bit too much. That night we went out on a trip to see the Northern Lights and, on stepping off the coach, I was literally starstruck. The sky, which I have always liked gazing into, was the most awesome picture of beauty I had ever seen.

The glory of creation stretched before me! I stood for ages staring into space, captivated by the sight and felt overwhelmed. When we got back on the coach, Angie told me how annoyed she was with me for ignoring her for large parts of the day. With hindsight, she was right, but at the time, I was in my own bubble and held hostage by Iceland's beauty. We argued terribly when we arrived back at our room, and I upset her. Eventually, it broke my heart and I tried to make it up to her with sweet words. I realised that I loved her so much, but some of her ways I found hard to deal with. As always, we kissed and made up.

A 'normal', one of Angie's favourite words to throw at me when she thought I was being outrageous, a year passed and into 2018 we headed. She had started to go through 'the change' as it is put and on a random night in February, texted me asking me to pick up sausage in batter and chips on my way down from my parents. I had been rushing around all day and didn't read the text properly, walking into the house with sausage and chips.

Suddenly, all hell let loose. She started screaming at me, crying, throwing the chips and sausage in its paper wrapping violently down on the kitchen worktop. At first, I joked, thinking she was messing around, but then I became alert to her seriousness. I lost my temper and stormed out, slamming the front door and heading back for my parents' house. My phone rang on the way, and I didn't answer, furious with her reaction over something so trivial. By the time I got there, she rang me again. I answered and told her to "F*** Off" before hanging up. At that moment, I wanted it to be over. I was no longer willing to put up with her mood swings and, in my mind, started planning my single life. The next morning, I woke up to find a text from her asking me to forgive her and saying she felt like 'the bitch from hell.' This melted my heart, and once again we resumed our love affair as if nothing had happened.

Easter that year, I had a text from Cez asking if we fancied coming to their church as there was an African children's choir visiting so we agreed. We sat together in the tiered section of Citychurch while a group of children, some as young as five, sang and ministered, testifying how Jesus had changed their lives. Their smiles of joy were enough to melt the hardest heart. I glanced at Angie and saw her wiping tears from her eyes, so I reached to put a comforting hand on her leg. She pushed it off in a 'don't touch me' kind of way. As we walked back to the car, I asked her if she enjoyed the service. "I want to go next week," she replied and I was ecstatic. We began to attend every week and loved it. We would discuss the bible at home but at first she told me, "I don't want to talk about God every day." After a few months of attending services, whilst the youth leader was preaching one morning, he called people to the front of the stage for prayer. Angie leapt from her seat and briskly walked down to the front of the church. I was shocked and went after her, knowing this was totally out of character for her. She had one of the stewards praying with her and I found myself standing alone, not actually wanting to be there. Afterwards, she told me she had thought that the preacher was speaking directly to her, "He kept looking at me," she said. "That was God speaking to you," I responded. In a church of hundreds of people, I can't imagine preachers aim their message at an individual they don't know. She had given her life to Jesus Christ that evening, and I was filled with the 'joy of the Lord'. This was a game-changer.

When a person accepts Christ's sacrifice for sin on the cross, they become a 'new creation'. The change in man is instant but the process of change, or sanctification as it is called, is a matter of surrendering certain parts of your life to God so that He can help you become more like Him. For the first few months, I saw little difference in Angie. Her arguments with Hannah stopped. She would not respond in the same way when they had normally clashed. Angie started keeping a journal, which I will use to reflect her feelings from now on.

Angie, "This is the start of a new life with God in it. God, hear my prayer and help me on my journey. I know it won't be easy but I give myself to you. Help me with my drinking. I struggle so hard to cut it back. It helps me to forget my past but I know now you can help me do it if I truly believe. Thank you for bringing Steve into my life. I know I have put up a wall where I wouldn't see his ways with you. It has taken me a long time to see that you are truly good. I know that you are out there helping my children and Kyle."

In August, we went on holiday to Venice. It is a romantic place, as anyone who has been there with a loved one will know. We shared a fantastic week together. No arguments, no differences of opinion, we just fell deeper in love with each other. I realised in this place that I wanted to spend the rest of my life with her. We had learned to love each other through thick and thin. One evening, we went to St. Mark's Square and, in a moment that still brings tears to my eyes, she told me that she couldn't imagine her life without me. I felt the same. Within a week of arriving home, she told me she could no longer sleep with me. I suggested we should get married, and she said, "You should have proposed in Venice, that would have been the romantic thing to do." I knew that, but hadn't thought of it then. On 6 September, I cooked a meal and set the table in the house. When she arrived home from work, I got down on one knee with a ring in one hand and champagne in the other and clumsily asked her to be my wife. She laughed at my awkwardness but accepted. We proceeded to plan our wedding, and I wanted it as soon as possible. I was struggling with not sleeping with her, even though I know I shouldn't. We set a date for 13 April 2019, and preparations began. She began to open up to me about her past, telling me intimate secrets she had never shared with anyone, and my love and admiration for her grew deeper and deeper.

Angie, "The secret of being transformed from a vulnerable victim to a victorious, loving person is found in the ability to open your past to someone responsible enough to share your weakness and pain. You don't have to keep living it, release it!"

She had no problem talking about her newfound faith with people and would often bring it into conversation with our family and friends. Her daughters noticed the new, relaxed version of their mother, still full of love, more so if that were possible, but her drinking was reduced.

She would still enjoy a glass of wine, but drew a line where she wouldn't have before. We read the word and prayed together, but there was still some of her old attitude. "Don't start preaching," she would say to me, basically telling me to be quiet.

Angie, "God, thank you for coming into my life. You have lifted my soul and I have never felt so blessed and safe as I do with you by my side. I will do my best to be a better person, but I know I will make mistakes. I will know different now with you in my life."

"I am valuable to God. I am somebody and I won't let another use me or abuse me and treat me like I'm nothing. Yes, I've been through some bad times. I've been hurt, I've been bent out of shape but the Lord touched me and loosed me and now I am glorifying God, and I'm not going back to where I came from."

"Reach out to God and rejoice as He watches over you and strengthens you like never before. Rejoice in Him, and He will anoint you with oil. The anointing of the Lord will be upon you if you truly believe."

"God, I know that I struggle sometimes with my faith, but please help me stay strong and guide me. I give myself to you, Lord and have faith that you will show me and guide me always."

Angie, March 2019, "Lasting change does not come through human effort, frustration, self-hatred, guilt or beating yourself up over your failures. It comes from having your mind renewed daily by the Word of God. If you're a consistent bible reader, you'll grow spiritually. As you agree with God and believe what He says in His word, you gradually begin to change. It just happens! You start to think differently, talk differently and act differently. But you must be patient because it's a process that develops in stages and you must learn to enjoy life whilst you're going through the transformation process. Many of us look like we're walking a tightrope rather than a pathway of peace. No, enjoy where you are on your way to where you're going! Don't waste all your 'now time' trying to rush into the future."

AMAZING GRACE

And so we were married on 13 April 2019, the photos remain of what a blessed day it was. Family and friends attended, and we celebrated our love for one another, thinking that we had many years spread out before us, building a life together and serving our Lord. We had a brief honeymoon after, a few days away, gifted by The Motley Crew and planned to go somewhere abroad in the summer. Emma was due to have her second baby, and the focus soon turned to that, our second grandchild. He was eventually born on 7 June and we rejoiced at the blessings in our life. Then Angie woke up one morning with a severe pain in her left hand. She went to the doctors and was told that it may be something to do with her liver, but they would run further tests. She came home crying and said to me, "I'm going to have to give up wine probably, that'll make you happy." It didn't. Further tests led to a scan and in early July, we were called to a specialist at Llandough Hospital. There, we were told that she had a couple of shadows on her lung and that they had to do a biopsy to determine what it was. Angie said that she had had pleurisy years before, and it may have been a result of that. We prayed and waited.

We were summoned back to the specialist shortly after and sat down to await her verdict. She was diagnosed with Sarcomatoid Mesothelioma. We asked what that was and what treatments were available, and what course of action we would be taking. I'll never forget the doctor's words. They came at me like Mohammed Ali's best punch. "Most people who contract this live, on average, 8 to 14…" years flashed through my mind. "…months," she finished. I remember exploding into tears. We retreated into a quiet room and wept uncontrollably together. Surely not? What about our faith? God wouldn't do this to us. We went straight to tell my parents and then to Cez and Michelle's, where we sat over coffee and wine, talking it over. Faith was the key, God heals people, and the bible is full of it, we would be praying for this.

Angie, "Lord, hear my prayer, listen to my cry for mercy. In your faithfulness and righteousness, come to my relief."

"For your name's sake, Lord, preserve my life. In your righteousness, bring me out of trouble."

"God, hear my prayer. Keep me strong at this troublesome time. Help us to overcome what lays ahead. With our faith and you by my side, I truly believe we will beat this together.

Thank you Lord, for coming into my life. I know I am not the best person but with you by my side, I can be. Thank you Lord, amen."

Telling people was hard. Our hearts broke as we felt their pain and it's impossible to know what to say to someone in this position. Our Christian brothers and sisters rallied to the cause positively. Word spread quickly, and faithful prayers went up to God in increasing numbers. I was confident that God would not let my newlywed wife die. I reasoned to myself and others that she would be healed for His glory. We had so much to do together for Him as I saw it, and He would be merciful.

Angie, "Lord, I am scared, please comfort me in this dark time. I cry out to you Lord. Help me to stay strong. I praise you Lord Almighty."

"God, O God, keep me strong and lift this darkness. I will not let the devil come back in, Lord. I worship you Lord. I praise you, Lord."

"Whatever your reason for this, Lord, I pray you keep me strong and help my children to understand and open their hearts to you. I would like to live a bit longer, Lord but that is in your hands, I know."

"I do feel cheated a bit as I've just come into my faith and have found such lovely friends and a strong husband. I have found some confidence which I lacked and understanding of you, Lord."

"As soon as you become aware that you're starting to worry and lose your sense of peace, take it to God immediately and leave it with Him. Don't give the devil time to work you over. The longer you wait, the greater his hold over you becomes. But I can't help thinking about it, I am a born worrier. Give it to God and start thinking of other things."

"Thank God that no matter how dark things seem, joy will always return. Weeping may endure for a night, but joy comes in the morning."

We went through chemotherapy briefly without success. Radiotherapy without success, and eventually immunotherapy. She was blessed with money from the government through solicitors. Her illness was asbestos-related and they began searching through her history for the cause. The money allowed her to book weekends and trips away with her family and friends, and we had some blessed times with her.

Angie, "Making memories, I'm aware that they are tinged with sadness."

Her health started to deteriorate. She had always had bundles of energy, but found it harder to do things as time went by and treatments were imposed. On 12 September, she posted a picture of her medication saying, "I'm ready...bring it on." On 26 October, she posted, "Whenever you do not understand what is happening in your life, just close your eyes, take a deep breath and say, 'God, I know it's your plan, just help me through it." She was ticking off birthdays one by one, keeping her private thoughts mainly to herself and her journal. Most of us can only guess what she was going through.

Angie, "Buying Hannah's birthday card today was so hard, as it's likely to be the last I give her. These things we all take for granted. I'm trying to hold on to every moment through the pain, but I feel like an emotional wreck at this moment in time."

"Sat here scared of what lays ahead. Losing control over what I will be able to do and stuff taken from me. My prayer is that it's not too bad for the girls and I stay strong and positive throughout and don't end up an emotional mess."

"Nights can be very hard, battling the dark moments and trying to get closer to our Father. I need more reassurance of God's faithful love and knowing He is with me always."

"It is good seeing Steve grow stronger in his faith and knowing that it is helping him greatly but he has to understand I'm in a different place. Plus, I'm the one who this is happening to, and it is very hard dealing with it every day. I'm scared of dying, I'm not ready. Keep praying for a miracle."

When I read these words, I realised that she had been keeping so much to herself. Although I feel we went through it together, she was so selfless in some things and it comes through here. She didn't want anyone else to feel her full pain and suffering. I was trying to keep my belief that God would heal her and refused to say any different, even though I had doubts myself. I would dismiss them as soon as they came to mind. In my weakness, I was still smoking marijuana, apologising to God and would feel a powerful conviction that I had to stop. We had a trip planned to Centre Parcs over the New Year, and I promised God that I would stop when we returned from that. We had always enjoyed our vices, even when we knew it was wrong in God's eyes, and she had largely stopped drinking wine as she wasn't enjoying it anymore.

Angie, "Many hours I have sat alone, crying at the thought of leaving my family so early. Wishing to see Hannah settled with children. Emma 'lol' married, yes, to Kyle! Kasia is becoming a beautiful, caring teenager and Momo running around the park kicking a football. Steve and I curled up on the settee with blankets, watching shit on TV. Me with my wine and Steve with his spliff."

We were heading for her favourite time of year, Christmas. All treatment was suspended and she prepared for what was going to be her last Christmas.

Angie, "Well Christmas is coming and I'm looking forward to the most precious time. I love family laughter and the time together. There's always something to sort out before but all is okay on the day. This year has been a year but we are strong as a family and will enjoy every moment and make more memories. Thank God I feel well and He is by my side to help and give me strength. Merry Christmas!"

She was doing all the usual things that she did at that time and more. Treasuring every catch-up with friends and making the most of the occasions, she felt well enough to do things. We had a wonderful Christmas and New Year away.

Angie, "Lovely Christmas and New Year away with the most precious people in my life. All had a lovely time and Kasia wanted to go back again. I was able to walk around as I was on the steroids. Done better than Steve! Watching my family have a lovely time, all getting on, laughing and talking, gives me peace that they will be there for one another through the good and bad times. So proud of my girls."

Into the New Year, and she was put on a new trial of immunotherapy.

Angie, "Haven't been too good these last two weeks. Breathing is really bad and scary. Trying to stay brave and calm but anxious about the drop in my well-being."

She started immunotherapy. The treatment was once a fortnight and after two courses, they took another scan. This was February, and it revealed that the tumour had nearly doubled in size since Christmas.

"The tumour has grown from 24 to 40 in a month. Hopefully, it is just a jump and it will slow down. God, please."

Her poor health was now very apparent in everything she did, which was becoming less and less. A wheelchair arrived at the house which she had been dreading, but she desperately wanted to do a trip to Harry Potter world with her daughters and Kasia. She managed it in early March and was so happy.

One subject that had come up when she was saved was baptism. She was frightened of standing up in front of people and, especially, of speaking in front of an audience. I had pushed for this to happen as quickly as possible back then but in the end, I had been forbidden to speak about it. It was something she had to decide for herself, and just before Christmas, I contacted Vaz, who was now a pastor, to see if we could arrange for it to happen. He was very busy but gave me a date, 29 March, when he could fit it in at his church. By early March, I realised that this was probably not going to be possible due to her health. She was having trouble just going upstairs and her energy levels had plummeted. He agreed to call over the house and do it in the bath.

Angie, "Time off from treatment. The pain has got a lot better. Thank you, God. Having a break for Christmas and New Year, then on to immunotherapy. It is time to be baptised and give my body and soul to Christ. I am ready now."

"When having chemo, I was all for getting baptised for the wrong reasons, for God to make me well. Now I am ready for the right reason. To give myself to the Lord once and for all."

On Thursday, 19 March 2020, Vaz came over. In the bedroom, where we had been for a few days, we read scripture, prayed and took communion. Her two daughters were present with her two grandchildren. Cez and Michelle watched on a live video feed. They had to send their apologies as Cez had a cold and didn't want to pass anything on but they sent a beautiful card which read;

> *"Angie, I will never forget the day we first met, you came over for dinner, and we hit it off straight away. Little did we both know what was going to unfold. Six years later, we have laughed...cried...done church...Alpha...salvation...Holy Spirit...engagement...marriage and now baptism...WOW! All of this in such a short space of time. Thank you for sharing the experience. You are an incredible woman. Thank you for your friendship, your love and care you have always shown me. You have been a true friend to Cez and our girls, and for that, I will always be grateful. With much love, Michelle."*

Vaz spoke of the blessings of God in people's lives and said that they were all in the room with her. We then went into the bathroom where he baptised her. Kasia filmed it on her phone and when you see the smile on her face when she comes out of the water, you realise that this was so important to her, a final hurdle. That morning, she couldn't move, and we prayed for one last miracle for God to give her strength. He answered. On 30 March, she left me for heaven.

WHAT'S SO FUNNY ABOUT PEACE, LOVE AND UNDERSTANDING

As I read her journal, which I found the day after she died, I rejoiced in God's strength in her life. The morning of her death, I picked up her word for the day, which is a daily reading and lesson Angie used to love to read, to find that it was about the comfort God gives when you lose a loved one. He has walked me through my experience, as He did Angie, and I made her promises I can never break. One of them was to stick with my faith until I die. That day, in the evening, I went to see Cez and Michelle. Cez said that he felt I should write a book about my life, and I went home and started it as it immediately made sense to me. I have always wanted to write, but have never known what about. I am writing this last page two weeks later, on the day of our first anniversary. We cried together and recounted memories of the wonderful times we'd had and how God brought Cez back from London. He never understood why and testified to the amazing things that led up to it happening, how God had 'opened doors'. I knew why. My prayer in all those years I spent in sin was, "How can I ever live for you again when my heart is so hard?" God, as He always does, answered. Not in a way that I would have chosen, but gracefully breaking me again, His way. Angie achieved everything she ever wanted to and told me at the end that she never dreamt that her life could be so complete. I'll leave the last words to her and hope that our story finds its destination in your heart.

Angie, "What a journey this last year has been! Easter, going to church and finding our Lord Jesus Christ who has changed my life completely. God knows what He was doing to prepare me for what lay ahead. The Lord is good. I don't know how I would cope without the support of my amazing family, friends and faith. They have held me up in my dark times as well as the good."

CONCLUDING THOUGHTS

As you now know, I believe God has taken me on an amazing path and allowed me to live it in a full and privileged way. I look back and see Him whisper to me at intervals in my life through books, strangers, angels and friends as I believe He does for all of us.

Everyone we ever meet plays a part in our lives and I have learned that by loving people, paying attention to their interests, it is easy to accumulate friends as we pass through planet Earth. I began years ago, seeing life as a kind of drama. People have their roles, some bigger than others. I've met many whom I have got to know well, but then suddenly, due to circumstance, vanish, never to be seen again. They leave their mark, though, and hopefully, I did on them.

It interests me that when you look back to the point of when you first meet someone, like me with Angie, for instance, you have no idea what they are going to mean to you in the future. So it is for all of us. I'd never have believed I was going to end up marrying her, let alone losing her within a year, and it's best that I didn't! But the impact we had on each other echoes into eternity. We can then treasure them in a part of our hearts and honour them in our future. I believe that this has made my grief easier, knowing that we completed a work in each other, enabling me to move on quickly with my life. Angie knew that as well. She told me that she knew I would cope far better with her dying than if it was the other way around. That is so humbling. She gave me her blessing to live my life 'to the full' again as long as I served God to the end of it and looked after her daughters. I hope you can see the freedom in that. Treasure everyone, take no one for granted. Serve God.

www.ingramcontent.com/pod-product-compliance
Lightning Source LLC
Chambersburg PA
CBHW060504080526
44584CB00015B/1548